Falling From The Sky

Falling From The Sky

Norm Sawyer

© 2025 Norm Sawyer
ISBN 10: 1-988226-74-0
ISBN 13: 978-1-988226-74-3

Cover Art: Kane Sawyer
Cover Graphics: Masud Choudhury

Published by

First Page Publishing
Kelowna, BC, Canada

Dedication

To Ever and Kacey. May God's grace and love cover you both, all the days of your life.

Contents

Foreword

In the spring of 2022, I stood at a crossroads—a man burdened by the weight of my own choices, desperate for meaning and direction. That was when I made the most life-changing decision of my journey: to proclaim Jesus Christ as my Lord and Savior. The path hasn't been easy, but it has been transformative. Walking in the Spirit as a child of God has challenged and refined me in ways I never imagined. It was by the sovereign grace of our Lord that on a quiet morning in 2024 at 5 a.m., I encountered Norm Sawyer at Global Gym. This was no coincidence; it was a divine appointment. Norm's presence reflected unwavering discipline, wisdom, and grace—the qualities of a man deeply rooted in Christ. From that moment, I knew I had met not just a leader but a shepherd in our community, someone uniquely equipped to guide others toward heaven's gates.

Reading Norm's Discipline is Freedom and his devotional collection, Every Day Is God's Day, awakened a thirst in me I hadn't known existed—a thirst for the purity, forgiveness, and wisdom found only in Jesus. Norm's gift lies in his ability to weave scripture with his own life's trials and triumphs, creating a bridge that connects God's word to the struggles and triumphs we all face. His writing speaks directly to the heart, offering encouragement to both the sinner and the steadfast believer.

Having walked through life's peaks and valleys—addiction, brokenness, fleeting successes, and profound failures—2024 became my year of complete surrender. Through Norm's books, I discovered clarity, hope, and the tools to navigate my faith journey. His insights are not just words on a page; they are living truths that point us all toward the only source of true peace and freedom: Jesus Christ.

His new book Falling From The Sky is yet another testament to Norm's God-given ability to lead others to the cross. It is an honor to write this foreword and to call Norm not just an author, but a mentor, leader, and friend. May this book bless and transform you as profoundly as Norm's work has for me and countless others. In His grace,

- Nicholas Mercier

Introduction

The Lord wants us to bring His kingdom to earth, as stated in His prayer, "Father, your Kingdom come, and your will be done on earth, as it is done in heaven." It was and is God's intention to have His kingdom flourish on this lost earth so that the restoration of all that was intended at creation would come to pass.

We are seated in heavenly places with Christ and have a better view of God's plan than the lost of this earth. The lost feel like they are falling from the sky because they are lost to God's friendship. Satan and his angels are the only ones to have ever fallen from the sky. Luke 10:18 **And He said to them, "I watched Satan fall from heaven like lightning.** Satan wants to bring fear into the hearts of the lost by saying that they are in a fallen state and can never rise above their present place of existence. Lies, lies, and more lies—no one who receives Jesus as Lord can fall from the sky. We are lifted up to sit with Him in Heavenly places.

We are more than conquerors and well-equipped to live a Godly life here and now. By learning the Word and walking in it day by day, our path to bringing God's kingdom here and now is possible; we only need to accept the assignment God gave us to make it happen.

Norm-Isms

When we fix the short-term habits, the long-term journey starts to flow, and victory starts teaching us how to win.

Let the art in your heart belong to God.

When you fall on your face, at least you are going forward.

Part One
Seated In Heaven

Sometimes the spiritual battles we go through can deceive us into thinking we will fall from our heavenly position and become self-absorbed souls trying to get back to the heavens when we are already there. The Word of the Lord states that we are now seated in Heavenly places with Christ, and have been given the authority to bring the blessings of God to the people of the world. Eph. 2:6 **And God raised us up with Christ and seated us with Him in the heavenly realms in Christ Jesus.** *Jesus has won the battle for the mind, soul, and body but we need to accept that gift and focus on what God has set in our hearts to do to bring about the kingdom of God on earth. This section looks at our struggles and the victories won through the finished work of the cross.*

Falling From The Sky

Isaiah 14:12 How you are fallen from heaven, O Lucifer, son of the morning! How you are cut down to the ground, You who weakened the nations!

When Satan fell from the sky, it was the result of God's judgment that would seal Satan's eternal existence of damnation. Luke 10:18 **Jesus replied, "I saw Satan fall from heaven like lightning.** The devil's fallen nature is beyond wretched misery; it is woefully desolate. Satan lives in an eternity of joyless wanderings, of emotional

1

hollowness, and is never able to understand the revelation or illumination of God's Word. Regardless of the truth set before him, his capacity to believe God's truth has been skewed by the corruption that burns within him. Eze. 28:18 **You have profaned your sanctuaries by the multitude of your iniquities and the enormity of your guilt, by the unrighteousness of your trade. Therefore I have brought forth a fire from your midst; it has consumed you, and I have reduced you to ashes upon the earth in the sight of all who looked at you.**

The devil is fighting a war on two fronts. He fights the church body of Christ, and he is fighting the judgmental flame of fire that God has set within him. A fire of consumption that cannot be quenched by any success Satan thinks he has won on this earth. No matter the millions of people he has killed or harmed over the centuries, there will never be a moment of satisfactory accomplishment. He will only be driven to deeper bitterness and forever reminded of the moment when he fell from the sky. His plan to get back into God's heavens will never come to fruition and Satan's last-place position will be his lot in eternity. How pathetic is his existence!

The marvel of being in Christ is that we are seated in heavenly places with our Lord. Our position is secured through Jesus who has welcomed us into His presence and invited us to sit with Him in His heavenly realm. Eph. 2:6 **And God raised us up with Christ and seated us with Him in the heavenly realms in Christ Jesus, 7 in order that in the coming ages He might display the surpassing riches of His grace, demonstrated by His kindness to us in Christ Jesus.**

We do not have to worry about falling from our heavenly place because through Jesus we have become heirs of Christ's holy inheritance, plus we have been made priests who now minister to our God in His kingdom. Rev. 1:6 **He has made us a Kingdom of priests for God his Father. All glory and power to Him forever and ever! Amen.** We are part of the eternal plan that God saw active within us before the foundations of the world.

When describing his visional dream of the ladder reaching into heaven, Jacob could not have imagined what we through Christ, now have access to. Gen. 28:12a **And he had a dream, and behold, a ladder was set up on the earth with its top reaching to heaven.** Jacob might have had an idea of the possibility of ascending into God's presence because he was in awe of his vision and convinced that he was standing at the gates of heaven. Therefore, he marked the location with a memorial stone. Gen. 28:18 **And Jacob rose up early in the morning, and took the stone that he had put for his pillows, and set it up for a pillar, and poured oil upon the top of it.** No longer are we required to look for a geographical location, tabernacle, or portal so to speak to find entrance into God's presence. We have eternal access through Christ our Lord no matter where we are in this universe.

Not only do we have a righteous permission to the presence of our Heavenly Father, but because of the cleansing blood of Jesus, we also have God's assurance that we will be with Him throughout eternity. Our door and gateway to heaven is through Jesus and Him only. John 10:9a **I am the door. If anyone enters in by Me, he will be saved.** We do not need to fear falling from the sky and losing the salvation of our souls. We are

3

seated in a heavenly place with Christ not because of anything we have done, but all because of what Jesus did for us through His sacrifice on the cross. Our sins have been washed away and our acceptance by God the Father is now our life to live. Eph. 2:8 **For it is by grace you have been saved, through faith—and this is not from yourselves, it is the gift of God.**

Falling from the sky or falling from grace is no longer a fear we need to be overwhelmed by. As we walk in obedience to the path God has set before us, we can enter His rest, where our souls were meant to live. Heb. 4:9 **There remains therefore a rest for the people of God. 10 For he who has entered His rest has himself also ceased from his works as God did from His.** The concept of living on earth while we are sitting in heaven is—in the natural— hard to think through. However, we have been made through the blood of Jesus supernatural beings, new creatures, and righteously accepted by God all because of the Love Jesus has for us. 2Cor. 5:17 **Therefore, if anyone is in Christ, he is a new creation. The old has passed away; behold, the new has come. Since the old part of our lives has passed away, let us stop going back to that life.** Let us enter and accept the new life God has given us so that we may live in peace with our God for now and evermore. Amos 3:3 **Can two walk together, except they be agreed?**

Questions:

What battles have you been fighting that need to be won right now?

What is your God-given strategy to win that battle?

Why Does God Hate Me?

Malachi 1:2 "I have always loved you," says the LORD. But you retort, "Really? How have you loved us?" And the LORD replies, "This is how I showed my love for you: I loved your ancestor Jacob, 3 but I rejected his brother, Esau, and devastated his hill country. I turned Esau's inheritance into a desert for jackals."

When someone feels hated by God, it is a hard place to come out of. The Psalmist Heman the Ezrahite wrote Psalm 88, and he seems to have been in a state of despair. Heman's thoughts and self-doubt are expressed out of anguish, and basically, he seems to be saying that God hates him. Of course, this was not true, but the feelings were in his heart and he felt raw and vexed of soul. Psalm 88:14 **LORD, why do you reject me? Why do you hide your face from me? 15 From my youth, I have been suffering and near death. I suffer your horrors; I am desperate. 16 Your wrath sweeps over me; your terrors destroy me. 17 They surround me like water all day long; they close in on me from every side.** Heman's groans can be felt, and his thoughts are filled with emotional despair which causes him to make a final statement of loss, and its reason hurts the heart to think about it. Psalm 88:18 **You have taken away my companions and loved ones. Darkness is my closest friend.**

How many people have felt like darkness was their closest friend while living out their faith in our Lord's salvation? History states that Heman was a grandson of Samuel the prophet, and was one of the composers of the music that was written for the Psalmist who had inspiredly written the Psalms. Heman would have seen firsthand and heard of the greatness of God. He would have participated in the praise that declared the wonders of God's goodness. Yet within this environment, he thought God had not favoured him in life nor had he felt God's friendship. To say that darkness was his only friend implies a feeling of being noticed but not seen, or not found to be valuable to God. How many times have we felt the sting of rejection, and wanted to scream out of frustration at the angst playing havoc in our hearts? Many a strong person would at this point, shout out loud, "Why does God hate Me"?

Whenever the statement is made, "God does not hate anyone," without fail, someone says, "God hated Esau but loved Jacob." It is interesting to see the word God uses to express this statement. The Word of God says that in effect, Esau hated his birthright. Gen. 25:34 **Then Jacob gave some bread and lentil stew to Esau, who ate and drank and then got up and went away. Thus Esau despised his birthright**. Some translations say that Esau showed contempt, scorned, slighted, belittled, and treated his right as firstborn with disdain. The Hebrew word for hate is sânê', (saw-nay') which suggests how Esau valued his birthright, and how he hated the responsibility of that birthright. When God says he hated Esau, God is using the same word sânê' that Esau used to belittle his birthright. God saw no value in Esau, the same way Esau saw no value in the gifting and responsibility God had given him through birth. Rom. **9:13 As it is written and forever remains written, "JACOB I LOVED (chose, protected, blessed), BUT ESAU I HATED (held in disregard compared to Jacob)."**

I can handle God not seeing any value in me, because I too, see no value in my existence compared to God's values. I can agree with God if He appeared to me and said, "Norm, I don't see any value in you." I could say, "Yes Lord, we are on the same page, I don't see any value in me either. However, Lord, I could never rise from You hating me in the sense of that word's usage today. I would be in the deepest despair of existence. For truly Lord, it would have been better that I not have been born." At least being of no value is a starting point for hope in the goodness of God, and the possibility to mature into a position of Godly value. I'm not saying that I am not valuable to my wife, children, friends and some segments of society. I may have earthly value, but it is reasonable to believe, I have no heavenly value at all. Therefore, the question might become, "Why do I feel God sees no value in me, rather than why does God hate me?"

I can see why God treated Esau in the manner He did because Esau treated the things of God with pure contempt. There was more than the contempt towards the birthright that Esau disdained. He also did not honour his parents and married outside of God's recommendation for righteous living. Esau married Hittite wives who were idol worshipers and would also bring grief to Isaac and Rebekah. Gen. **26:34 At the age of forty, Esau married two Hittite wives: Judith, the daughter of Beeri, and Basemath, the daughter of Elon. 35 But Esau's wives made life miserable for**

7

Isaac and Rebekah. No matter the dispensation God is instructing His people within, the wages of sin are still death, disintegration, and dissipation of character and soul. Esau chose to hate God and what God valued, and God returned to Esau what he had sown in life. Mal. 1:3b **I turned Esau's inheritance into a desert for jackals.**

Many people feel a burning stare of God's expectation upon their lives and falsely interpret that feeling into thinking they are hated. The dilemma they are facing is that they are trying to measure up to the Almighty within their fragile existence and self-righteousness. However, God is love and has given us His holy gift in Jesus Christ to be able to come home to Him. The Psalmist Heman, and the many people in the Bible who felt like they had fallen short of God's love, protection, or standard had simply met the reality that God's righteousness is beyond what anyone can imagine it to be. There is nothing on Earth or in the universe to compare God's righteousness to, nor has anyone understood within the realm of our existence the fullness of its grace. We all fall short of the Lord's perfection. Only through Christ can we start life's holy journey. Even within a lifetime of walking with the Lord will still be required to realize that we have nothing to offer toward God's salvation plan except to receive that eternal grace-filled gift He has offered us. It is all God and Him alone who brings us along into His holy existence.

Timothy Keller said, "We tend to put much emphasis on the quality of our faith rather than the object of our faith." With this in mind, we might take responsibility for the question and ask, "Why do I hate myself, and blame that feeling on God?" Perhaps the solipsistic nature of our souls causes us to seek the reassurance of salvation in the performance of our faith, rather than the object of our faith which is Christ the Lord. Maybe it is because we cannot resist our willingness to be in control of God that we cannot see our desperate need for His deliverance. Like the Apostle Paul, we wrestle with our inner man as we conform to the image of Christ, crucifying our flesh day after day. Rom. 7:15 **For I do not understand my own actions I am baffled and bewildered by them. I do not practice what I want to do, but I am doing the very thing I hate and yielding to my human nature, my worldliness—my sinful capacity.**

As I accept my need to be in God's presence while being fully immersed in the work of His sacrifice, I hope to come into a mature measure of authentic faith and ask, "Why does God love me?" This is a far better question to resolve in my soul. The answers are much more faith and soul-building rather than the never-ending questions of dark sayings that ask, "Why does God hate me? I think the devil would be far too pleased to fill you in on the many reasons that question invokes. No, Saints, we need to find our rest and assurance in the finished work of the cross and accept the love it took for Jesus to take our deserved place on that cross. God does not hate you, He loves you and He will bring you through difficult suffering, growing heart pains, and higher expectations to prove His love for you, and one day you will hear Him say, "Well done, faithful friend." May we all hang on to these words of life. John 3:16 **For God loved the world so much that he gave His one and only Son, so that everyone who believes in Him will not perish but have eternal life.**

Questions:

Have you ever felt like God was not hearing your prayers?

_____

What did you do about connecting with God's love?

_____

Shame Speaks Loudly

Hebrews 12:2 Looking unto Jesus the author and finisher of our faith; who for the joy that was set before him endured the cross, despising the shame, and is set down at the right hand of the throne of God.

Martin Luther described the effects of sin within man this way: "Sin is man curved in upon himself." How true that sin and the choosing to participate in it is the result of curving inward to the point that nothing outside of yourself matters. The dark and mercurial nature of sin breeds self-condemnation within our souls. The more iniquitous we become, the deeper we twist inward to the core of selfishness, and the more opportunity for shame to take root dictating our choices going forward. No wonder people who suffer relentless shame experience continual confusion and feel like the inner parts of their souls are so twisted they can find no peace. Psalm 44:15 **My confusion is continually before me, and the shame of my face hath covered me.**

These are only my thoughts on the high rates of suicide, and the feelings of absolute rejection and abandonment that many are living through. These manifestations of the deep wounds occurring in people's souls might be attributed to the levels of shame they are experiencing in their daily lives. When I talk with people in a counselling session, the theme that recurs most often about unresolved shame is normally the result of unconfessed sin. The abortion that no one in the family knows about haunts the soul of the young lady who went through the procedure on her own. The loss of money that was needed to feed his family that he wasted on a gambling website fills him with dread having to face and confess this addiction to his wife. The pride within man is beyond understanding in some cases. Prov. 11:2 **When pride comes, then comes shame; but with the humble is wisdom**. The cheating spouse, the thieving son, and the many other sins that cause a man to hide in shame are endless.

I have heard many of these tearful confessions over the years, and I am convinced that only Jesus can heal and turn around the sinful mess we try to hide throughout our lives. The pride of life knows no boundaries and is not prejudiced as to who it manipulates. 1John 2:16 **For all that is in the world, the lust of the flesh and the lust of the eyes and the boastful pride of life, is not from the Father, but is from the world**. After these sins have taken root in people's hearts, shame will often accompany them as they go through the agony of their choices. There is a desire within the confused soul to bring about some restitution because the weight of the shame is palpable. Therein is the rub. We want to build our own sacrificial altars that we think are acceptable to

God. Life's pride interferes with what Christ has already put in place for the remission of our sins and the healing of our shame. 2Cor. 5:21 **For God made Christ, who never sinned, to be the offering for our sin, so that we could be made right with God through Christ.**

How does shame make us want to get in God's way and try to fix the torment we are experiencing? Or what would make us go in the opposite direction and hide our shame by living a secretive life always pretending everything is fine? The enemy of our soul puts a lot of stock in spewing out the reasons why we should pick up the shame we once left at the cross. There are many sins from my past that God has forgiven me for through the blood of Jesus, but Satan tries to trick me into picking up the shame of those old sins. What power is there in shame that makes us forget the forgiving grace God lavished on us when we confessed our sins the first time? Yes, I am sorry for the hurts and results of my selfish choices, but I need to remember that the condemnation and shame of those sins have also been washed in the blood of Jesus. Rom. 8:1 **Therefore there is now no condemnation [no guilty verdict, no punishment] for those who are in Christ Jesus [who believe in Him as personal Lord and Savior].**

You would think that after many centuries of the Lord's forgiving grace being poured upon the Christians of the earth, Satan would become discouraged at continually accusing us of what God has already forgiven us for. The pathetic thing is that Satan cannot be anything other than his nature which is to rob, kill, destroy and lie about everything that God graciously does for us. No wonder the Lord tells us that the weapons of this spiritual warfare are not of this world. We need the weapons of God's kingdom to defeat the shameful accusatory whisperings that come from hell. 2Cor. 10:4 **For the weapons of our warfare are not human weapons, but are made powerful by God for tearing down strongholds.** We tear down arguments. Shame is Satan's weapon against those who are having a hard time in life and the blood of Jesus is our weapon that destroyed the works of the enemy.

What are you ashamed of? What has Satan been accusing you of that has already been covered by the blood of Jesus? What shameful event does the devil keep bringing up in your face that makes you weak in your knees and forgetful that God's grace has covered all your shameful sins with His perfect sacrifice through Christ? The resolve of faith that you need to declare over these past forgiven events will need to be expressed again and again until the enemy flees from you in fear. James 4:7 **Submit yourselves, then, to God. Resist the devil, and he will flee from you.**

Faith in the blood and sacrifice of the cross of Jesus Christ is the only way to conquer the loud accusations that shame screams at us. As we believe God for the healing within our souls and we put the reasons for our past shame under the blood of our Saviour, let us get a picture of Satan being hurled down into hell where he will have no one but himself to accuse. He will be eternally stuck in the torture of his shame. Talk about plans backfiring. Rev. 12:10 **Then I heard a loud voice in heaven say: "Now have come the salvation and the power and the kingdom of our God, and the authority of His Messiah. For the accuser of our brothers and sisters, who accuses them before our God day and night, has been hurled down.** Shame may speak loudly, but the Lord's grace speaks louder and will keep speaking throughout eternity.

Question:

What is holding you back from taking the next step toward handing over all your burdens to the Lord?

The Burden Of Habakkuk

Habakkuk 1:2 How long, LORD, must I call for help, but you do not listen? Or cry out to you, "Violence!" but you do not save? 3 Why do you make me look at injustice? Why do you tolerate wrongdoing? Destruction and violence are before me; there is strife, and conflict abounds. 4 Therefore the law is paralyzed, and justice never prevails. The wicked hem in the righteous, so that justice is perverted.

I have had a few disturbing conversations with Christians (most of them in my age range) who have lost hope in their faith and God's ability to change the condition of what they see as an incurable insanity that is crisscrossing the world like a pandemic. To them, God looks like an absentee landlord who has allowed the rats and vermin of the earth to flourish and leave His people in want. These people want to die and go to their eternal home and be rid of it all. They want off this planet being run by despots, dictators, and idiots. They have no energy left to listen to another rah rah rah sermon about how good God is! The desperation is palpable and my heart is crushed as I hear these people describe their pain.

I do not claim to understand all their pain and reasons for so much despair, but I know that many of us have all had some thoughts along the lines they are expressing. I found these same anxieties in the book of Habakkuk. He is saying the same thing and lamenting similar feelings from many years ago. What many of the world's population is going through, is what I call The Burden Of Habakkuk. Hab. 1:2 **How long, LORD, must I call for help, but you do not listen? Or cry out to you, "Violence!" but you do not save? 3 Why do you make me look at injustice? Why do you tolerate wrongdoing? Destruction and violence are before me; there is strife, and conflict abounds. 4 Therefore the law is paralyzed, and justice never prevails. The wicked hem in the righteous, so that justice is perverted.**

As we can see, there is nothing new under the sun. These feelings and thoughts have been with us for a long time. One of our vulnerabilities is that we don't like what we don't understand. Even on our best days we will never be Jesus, nor understand the full plan of God. The question we need to ask is, how have we become so easily discouraged and offended? Maybe it is how we have presented the Bible and the Saviour this book is about. We get offended by those who reject our explanation of Jesus because of how we present Him culturally. These are only my thoughts. I find that we preach the accepting of Jesus, and His salvation from our cultural perspective more than the illumination of God's Word. If the Jesus we teach does not reach the cultural idea of another person then we are open to being offended because our Jesus has been rejected and that reflects on us. Our narrow-minded views can create a solipsistic idea of who God is and when we see the world's destruction we think God has left the planet, even though He resides in our hearts.

We only need to look at the thousands of self-proclaimed YouTube prophets who always have a prophetic warning for America. Isn't it interesting that there is never a warning from God for Russia that its dictator is killing his neighbouring countrymen at will and jailing his people for not agreeing with his scorched earth plan? Or there is no prophetic warning for North Korea where that despot is murdering his own citizens. No, just warnings to America. Not a warning to the tyrant leading Syria who has starved off his people and killed them at will because they wanted to be free. No warnings to Africa where murder and slavery still abound. Nor warnings to Canada, Argentina, Switzerland or England. No, Saints, it's just the good old USA who gets all of God's warnings of doom and gloom according to these YouTube prophets because the people of America are not voting for some shallow soul they deem electable in God's eyes. Forgive my sarcasm, but I know many of you are thinking what I am saying, and maybe we have been listening to too many online ministries and not digging into the Word of God for ourselves. No wonder there is no hope on the horizon for common sense.

I realize that what I do online can affect people's hearts and I recommend that anyone who reads my blogs, books, or articles and watches my videos check the scriptures and prove that my work lines up with the Word of God. Just because the minister is a trusted person, does not mean we take everything they say at face value. Even the Apostle Paul (who wrote most of the New Testament) was checked and rechecked against the Word of God by the Bereans. Acts 17:11 **Now the Berean Jews were of more noble character than those in Thessalonica, for they received the message with great eagerness and examined the Scriptures every day to see if what Paul said was true.** We have been too long complacent in handing over our unquestioning trust to the evangelical television machine that has become flawed and in some cases, corrupted.

Many complex and deep revelations in God's Word cannot all be dumbed down to simple reductionism. Yes, through the Holy Spirit, Christ's doctrines can be understood, when we allow the Lord to lead our lives. However, we cannot explain all the mysteries of the Godhead to people who do not take time to be with the Lord nor care what the Lord has offered mankind. We need the teaching and guidance of the Holy Spirit to find the peace of God that truly meets our inner heart's needs, and we need to keep our souls coming back into God's presence to be renewed afresh in the Holy Spirit. 1Cor. 2:14 **The person without the Spirit does not accept the things that come from the Spirit of God but considers them foolishness, and cannot understand them because they are discerned only through the Spirit.** After an encounter with the Spirit of God in our prayer time, we can then begin to understand the complexities that are going on in this world. With God's help, we will have the understanding to pray for the said issues that are a concern to our spirit, and soon we will see and know in our hearts that our God is not an absentee landlord, but is truly upon the throne of our hearts.

We were not saved by the stylism of Christianity nor by a rote formulaic arrangement of words. We are saved by faith in the blood of Jesus that was spilt on the cross, and we were saved by accepting His sacrifice only. As the burden of Habakkuk spreads throughout the world, let us first talk with God about all the evil that concerns us and ask Him what part of the burden He would like us to pray for so that God can heal that situation. God is not moved by needs, He is moved by faith. Remember, our lives are faith-driven and spiritually discerned. When we walk in the spirit, we will not kowtow to the flesh nor see every terrible thing that happens as a disaster that will last forever. Gal. 5:16 **But I say, walk by the Spirit, and you will not gratify the desires of the flesh.** Let us take our place on the prayer wall and use the weapons of our warfare to take down the strongholds that are corrupting the world. Jesus is Lord! Father God, help all the Saints who have lost hope to find it again in Your love for them. Amen!

Question:

Do you feel powerless in this world or have you found God's rest?

Even Dogs Get Crumbs

Matthew 15:26 And He answered and said, "It is not good to take the children's bread and throw it to the dogs."27 But she said, "Yes, Lord; but even

the dogs feed on the crumbs which fall from their masters' table."

The Syrophoenician woman who had felt the class difference of her day and might have felt treated like a dog through life, found hope in Jesus. It was a small hope, a shot in the dark hope, but hope nonetheless. She had problems like many people today. She said it plainly. Matt.15:22b **"Have mercy on me, Lord, Son of David! My daughter is severely tormented by a demon."** In the same way that many people today are possessed and tormented by addictions, sickness, poverty, and trial after trial are worn out, a miracle is needed. Everyone needs a crumb of peace and mercy. People may be living in some of the hardest dog days they have experienced in life so far. The misery of life is all around us and some allow the circumstances of misfortune to beat them down, and others use the same circumstances to get up and give life another try. Prov. 24:16 **For a righteous man may fall seven times and rise again, but the wicked shall fall by calamity.**

Calamity is a good word to explain the whirlwind of emotions, fears, and shrapnel flying through the lives of many. These poor souls look up to heaven and scream, "How about a break here!" in the hope of getting out of the quagmire of life's challenges and finding a morsel of peace. To these people, the contrast is a hard image to take in when living in a world so full of potential possibilities but just out of reach for the downcast. There is an understanding within every person's heart that life should be lived to the fullest, but many seem to hit a wall of exhaustion that prohibits them from taking what they need to experience something better. They are fighting a battle on two fronts—the struggle of everyday life that can be seen, and invisible phantoms that cannot be seen but only felt in the realm of the spirit. Mental prisons become their place of residence, and a crushed spirit keeps them in a state of hopelessness.

Whenever I see the homeless and the street dwellers shuffling along, I often think of what my friend Jim says. "We are all just one brain injury away from ending up in their shoes, We could find ourselves so easily living like they are because many people are just one paycheque away from ending up on the street." I agree with Jim, and when I think of his words of sympathetic understanding, I send a flare-prayer to God for our society which is going through difficult times. Many are looking for a small piece of momentary peace and rest, so they can be released from the world's pressures crushing down upon its citizens.

Let me assure you, there is much more than just crumbs of deliverance available from God. There is a whole banquet of mercy, provision, and forgiveness waiting for anyone who desires to sit at the Lord's table and indulge in a full measure of God's redemption. Psalm 23:5 **You prepare a feast for me in the presence of my enemies. You honour me by anointing my head with oil. My cup overflows with blessings**. God is generous and full of grace and mercy wanting no one to be lost. The Lord has gone through a lot of trouble over the centuries to give anyone who calls upon His name a personal audience to be affirmed as the apple of God's eye, and to be washed of all their sins and shortcomings. God's table is set, we only need to sit down and eat a full range of the Lord's heavenly delights. Psalm 34:8 **Taste and see that the LORD is good; blessed is the man who takes refuge in Him!**

When Peter and John came across the paralyzed man who was begging for a few crumbs to get by for the day, Peter, through the Holy Spirit, gave him a full meal of God's goodness. Peter did not have gold and silver to meet a temporary need but he had the power of God's gracious healing that would give this man a whole new life. Acts 3:6 **But Peter said, "I have no silver and gold, but what I do have I give to you. In the name of Jesus Christ of Nazareth, rise up and walk!"** For all of his life, he had been paralyzed, and in a moment of God's amazing grace, he was made whole and walked into the temple praising God. He did not get a crumb from God, he got a holy filling that touched his body, soul and spirit. True hope and joy had moved into his heart and life.

We who have received Jesus Christ as our personal Lord and Saviour also have this glorious power within each one of us. The issue may be that we have not stepped forward by faith to proclaim who lives within our hearts. The Lord said we would do great work in His name. John 14:12 **Truly, truly, I say to you, the one believing in Me, the works that I do, also he will do. And he will do greater than these, because I am going to the Father.** We do not need to give out crumbs as if the kingdom of God lacks resources or is on a budget because it lacks funding. The Lord owns the universe and the fullness thereof, and all of what is in the universe is at our disposal for the blessing of mankind. The generous blessings of God are for anyone who looks to God for mercy and the salvation of their lives. The Lord is the only Saviour to meet every mental need, physical demand, or soul-filling purpose. Isa. 43:11 **I, yes I, am the LORD, and there is no Savior but**

Me. We do not need to be dogs begging for crumbs at the Lord's table, but by faith in Christ, we can be sons and daughters who belong to the Lord's family living in the love God has for us. We can ask Jesus for all that we need according to the will of the Father and live in the assurance of His grace.

The choice is ours. We can approach God begging like a slave for crumbs or we can approach our Abba Father who loves and takes care of His sons and daughters. Rom. 8:15 **For you did not receive the spirit of slavery to fall back into fear, but you have received the Spirit of adoption as sons, by whom we cry, "Abba! Father!"** Only God can fix the mess we have made of our lives. May we all have the heart to trust what God is doing in our souls, and may we be the hand extended that He uses to bring His mercy to a troubled and broken society.

Question:

Do you feel less than who God says you are? If so, what do you need to accept by faith to overcome this feeling?

Picking Scabs

Leviticus 13:2 When a man has on the skin of his body a swelling, a scab, or a bright spot, and it becomes on the skin of his body like a leprous sore, then he shall be brought to Aaron the priest or to one of his sons the priests.

Why do some people only see, or choose to only focus on the mistakes a person makes? Why do some take on the role of a Levitical priest searching for the scabs that can disqualify a person from the sheepfold? These leprous spot hunters seem unhappy if they cannot find a scab to pick off of the character of the person they are judging. Doesn't love say to look for the best in each other? 1Cor. 13:7a **Love bears all things regardless of what comes, believes all things looking for the best in each one.** Shouldn't we try to clean up the boards in our eyes before we judge others' scars and scabs? Matt. 7:5 **You hypocrite, first take the plank out of your own eye, and then you will see clearly to remove the speck from your brother's eye.**

I was talking with a brother in the Lord who was criticizing a few ministries because these ministers did not believe the exact way he believed. This brother was continually picking at everything these ministers were saying and doing. I said, "How can you nullify their total ministry because of one view of doctrine (not affecting salvation in Christ) that you do not agree with?" I said, "They are not teaching another way of salvation outside of Jesus. They have a difference in how they pray during water baptism. How can you be so put out with that?" I realized that picking scabs on others had become this person's pastime. I find this attitude to be the reasoning behind those who insist on justice in all situations while grace remains in the background only to be called upon when the person judging needs mercy.

The wounds we acquire, as we walk toward our eternity, are many. Why add to the burden of someone's life who is walking at a different pace or level of maturity in their faith than you are? We all seek and need mercy but we are too fast to dispense and demand justice. When we are all standing before the Lord on that great day, I am sure we will all be pleading the blood of Jesus so that the full measure of God's mercy will be poured out on us. I'm convinced you will not be demanding that justice be used to judge your life in the same way you demanded justice toward everyone you met. Hos. 10:12 **Sow righteousness for yourselves, reap the fruit of unfailing love, and break up your unplowed ground; for it is time to seek the LORD, until he comes and showers his righteousness on you.** Yes, Lord, pour down YOUR righteous grace on me, and not the justice I deserve.

When I catch myself picking scabs, I quickly start looking at the root of these thoughts that have made their way to the forefront of my mind. I ask myself, "Am I being honest in my evaluation, or am I being petty? Is what I'm thinking coming out of a spirit of offence, or am I picking up something in the spirit that I am to pray about?" It is easy to start following the crowd if we do not take captive the thoughts that flow through our minds and hearts. One minute the people are singing "Hallelujah in the highest," and the next minute the same people are screaming, "Crucify Him!" Who do you want to be, the singer, or the screamer? James 3:10 **Out of the same mouth come praise and cursing. My brothers and sisters, this should not be. 11 Does a spring pour out sweet and bitter water from the same opening?**

As long as we are on this side of eternity, there will be an ample amount of scabs to pick from the people of this earth. We are never going to get it all right all the time. Without Jesus guiding our thoughts and hearts we will be plagued by the leprosy of man's filthiness. It was at the cross where Jesus was nailed that our sicknesses, diseases, and leprous thoughts were nailed with Him. We now have the Holy Spirit who comes and convicts us of the sins that must be cleaned up with the blood of Jesus. Our Saviour, Jesus, is our high priest who is the only one who determines our cleanliness of heart. Heb. 4:14 **Therefore having a great high priest having passed through the heavens, Jesus, the Son of God, we should hold firmly to our confession.**

Lev. 13:2 **When a man has on the skin of his body a swelling, a scab, or a bright spot, and it becomes on the skin of his body like a leprous sore, then he shall be brought to Aaron the priest or to one of his sons the priests.** It is the Lord Jesus who now inspects us and declares us to be the righteousness of God in Christ, and leads us to His pasture. As the Lord puts His hands on our lives to heal and cleanse us from the scars, rashes, and spots of sin, we can now walk in the fullness of His righteousness. Let us remember that we are all headed toward eternity and instead of picking each other apart, let's pray honourably for each other to finish the race God has set before us. Heavenly Father, thank you, for your grace.

Questions:

Is it difficult for you to see the best in others?

_____

Are you jealous when others get what they pray for and you have been finding no answers from God?

My Stony Heart

Ezekiel 36:26 Moreover, I will give you a new heart and put a new spirit within you, and I will remove the heart of stone from your flesh and give you a heart of flesh. 27 I will put my Spirit within you and cause you to walk in My statutes, and you will keep My ordinances and do them.

What a transformative promise the Lord has given us through Christ our Lord. God loudly proclaims, "I will give you a new heart!" Such a miraculous feat and declaration of God's power. The extent of what God did may never be clearly understood until we stand in His infinite presence. The Lord transforms the heart of a man who walks throughout life with free will. Our God, with one perfect sacrifice through Christ, which can never be matched by any of the good works, best intentions, or sacrifices made throughout the history of mankind has secured for us an eternal blessing. Not only did God give us a new heart, but He made a way for us to walk in His holy statutes and ordinances by giving us His Spirit. Eze. 36:27 **I will put my Spirit within you and cause you to walk in My statutes, and you will keep My ordinances and do them.**

Those who have accepted Jesus as their Lord have become the recipients of a heart that seeks and runs after

God. The only fly in this precious ointment is that we are the only ones who can mess this up. Satan can tempt and deceive people's hearts, but it is still a person's choice to break fellowship with God. When our hearts are absent from intimacy within our relationship with the Lord, we can become habituated to the routine of religious activity. At this point, our hearts are likely to become stony and callous. In a short time, we can become selfish and mean by showing no sympathy or regard for others. Matt. 15:8 **These people honour me with their lips, but their hearts are far from me.** Allowing the Holy Spirit to continually lead and direct our ways will keep our hearts soft and attentive to the perfect love God has lavished upon us.

When God encountered Saul on the road to Damascus, The Lord gave Saul a new heart that would change his life from the inside out. Here was a man who zealously condemned Christians to death, but then became the man who gave his life for the gospel of Jesus Christ. Phil. 2:17 **But even if I am poured out as a drink offering on the sacrificial service of your faith, I am glad and rejoice with all of you.** Saul's heart of stone had been cracked open by the power of the Holy Spirit which allowed Jesus Christ to rule and reign in him for the rest of his life. What a testimony of God's goodness and grace.

Jesus had a heart that was always submitted to God the Father. He continually pointed out that the issues and problems the people were going through were often the result of what was in their hearts. Luke 6:45 **A good man brings good things out of the good stored up in his heart, and an evil man brings evil things out** of the evil stored up in his heart. **For the mouth speaks what the heart is full of.** Jesus consistently spoke to the stony heart condition that was prevalent in the religious leaders and priests of the day. He called out their hypocrisy by showing them that what was coming out of their hearts were laws and rules that they could not keep but were expected to be kept by the people they ruled over. Matt. 23:4 **They tie up heavy, cumbersome loads and put them on other people's shoulders, but they themselves are not willing to lift a finger to move them.** The hearts of the Pharisees had lost compassion for the hearts of the people.

I find that when I become aware of a stony heart beginning to manifest in my life is often after I have been offended by something or have become complacent in my dedication to what God asks of me. If I have been hurt or treated unkindly I notice that gristle starts to form on the edges of my heart. My reaction to my clogged-up heart begins to cause self-preservation and the agenda to protect myself moves to the front of my mind. Thank God for the warning from the Holy Spirit who points to these unwelcomed symptoms and preps me for an operation by the Lord as fast as repentance comes through my mouth. 1John 1:8 **If we confess our sins, He is faithful and just to forgive us our sins, and to cleanse us from all unrighteousness.**

Even the most hard-hearted person can receive a holy recreated heart from God if they want one. We know this battle for the heart that is going on in the Heavenly realm, is the crux of the matter. Satan would not be going after the Word of God in our hearts if it were not so important for our ability to have a heart of flesh that pursues God. Mark 4:15 **Some people are** like seed along the path, where the word is sown. As soon as they hear it, Satan comes and takes away the word that was sown in them. Let us be clean in our hearts by pleading the blood of Jesus, and remain soft-hearted through the power of the Holy Spirit. Let us be grateful to our Heavenly Father for His amazing miracle of eternal life that He placed within our souls. Yes, Lord, by Your grace, give us a heart of flesh and a love that runs after You, and You only. This is what we all secretly want and need.

Questions:

What were the two major changes that took place in your heart after you received Jesus as Lord?

1.————————————————————

2.————————————————————

What was it you found in Jesus that brought the softening of your soul?

————————————————————————

The Darkness Of Discontentment

Malachi 3:13 "You have criticized me sharply," says the LORD, "but you ask, 'How have we criticized you?' 14 You have said, 'It is useless to serve God. How have we been helped by keeping

his requirements and going about like mourners before the LORD who rules over all?

I asked God how the people of North America had become so discontented with their lives and all they had. The majority of the population has so many creature comforts available to most people in this part of the world. Yet people's hearts have very little peace, joy, and contentment. Not only is there no gratitude for what they have, but there seems to be minimal effort to find something to be grateful for. Like entitled petulant children, refusing to be impressed with anything the Lord has done for them, they sit back and wonder why they have such a pusillanimous relationship with God. Mal. 3:14 **You have said, 'It is useless to serve God. How have we been helped by keeping his requirements and going about like mourners before the LORD who rules over all?**

Instead of seeing Jesus as the gift of life God gave us, these ingrates can find nothing good in God and accuse Him of the unhappiness they are manifesting. They talk a good Christian talk and even have the Christianese down to a fine art, but they do not come to the cross to acknowledge their need for the Saviour nor to be healed of their ungratefulness. 2Tim. 3:5 **They will act religious, but they will reject the power that could make them godly. Stay away from people like that!** We need to pray that Jesus can be seen in times of ungratefulness. This darkness is an attack from the enemy of our soul. Satan comes to rob, kill, and destroy a person's grateful heart. Satan knows that if we become complainers, we will lose the peace that comes through the gratitude and thankfulness we offer God.

The children of Israel lost so much because of their murmuring and ungrateful hearts toward their God who had delivered them from slavery. Num. 21:5 **The people spoke against God and Moses: "Why have you led us up from Egypt to die in the wilderness? There is no bread or water, and we detest this wretched food!" 6 Then the LORD sent poisonous snakes among the people, and they bit them so that many Israelites died.** Ouch! This same venom is still showing itself through the murmuring of discontentment within the hearts of mankind. Whether it be in the world or the church, this darkness makes its way like a rising fog that obscures the beauty and grace God has given us. The noise of discontentment is blocking the voice of the Lord who is saying, "Be still and know that I Am your God." How dark must it get before we crave the light of the Lord's forgiving grace?

In the book of Numbers chapter sixteen, Korah and his mob of discontents were all talking the talk of the day. Like misguided politicians, they were currying favour from the unhappy constituents to become leaders instead of putting up with the way Moses was leading. They used phrases like, "We are people of Renown, we are a holy community, why can't we take our religion and do it our way? Why are we not as equal as you, Moses?" Num. 16:3 **They came together against Moses and Aaron and told them, "You have gone too far! Everyone in the entire community is holy, and the LORD is among them. Why then do you exalt yourselves above the LORD's assembly?"** Discontented hearts and lives breeds jealousy and covetousness. When Moses heard this he went to his knees and buried his face under God's hand of judgment. Moses then explained to Korah that tomorrow we will stand before God and we will let Him choose who He wants to lead the people of Israel.

Epictetus wrote: *It is impossible for a man to learn what he already thinks he knows.* I think God and Moses were giving Korah and all his followers a day to think about their ungratefulness towards God and how He wanted leadership to be done. They all had a day to repent and become grateful for what they had. These Levites had a ministry to perform but were not thankful to God for what they had and now wanted the holy office of the priesthood. They wanted everything they saw Moses walking in. Their reason for the hostile takeover was that Moses had not yet brought them to the land of milk and honey, and everything was taking too long. Num. 16:14a **What's more, you haven't brought us into another land flowing with milk and honey. You haven't given us a new homeland with fields and vineyards**.

The standoff that had come to a breaking point was about to be cleared up by God. Those of you who are with Korah stand over there, and those of you who are with my servant Moses stand over here. Num. 16:32 **The earth opened its mouth and swallowed them and their households, all Korah's people, and all their possessions. 33 They went down alive into Sheol with all that belonged to them. The earth closed over them, and they vanished from the assembly**. God will judge our thankless hearts. We are so blessed to be on this side of the cross where Jesus has paid for our sins of murmuring, complaining, thanklessness, and all the resentment that goes with these sins of ungratefulness.

If you have become resentful, disgruntled, and aggrieved with your walk in the faith then bring Jesus back into your daily prayers. Only Jesus can break the darkness that envelops a selfish soul. We should not fool ourselves into thinking that a bit of complaining about God's ways will go unnoticed. The results will show up in our character, and out of the heart, the mouth will speak what comes out of it. If our hearts are full of gratitude towards God, then that is what will come out. As Paul says, we should think about the good things God has for us, and live in the fullness of His peace. Let us be grateful and think about the good things God has blessed us with. Phil. 4:8 **Finally, brothers, whatever is true, whatever is honorable, whatever is just, whatever is pure, whatever is lovely, whatever is commendable, if there is any excellence, if there is anything worthy of praise, think about these things**.

Questions:

How often do you take time to thank God for the blessings in your life?

_____

Do you find it hard to find things to be grateful for, or does giving thanks to God come easy to you?

_____

The Weight Of The World

Matthew 11:28 Come to me, all who labour and are heavy laden, and I will give you rest. 12 Take my yoke upon you, and learn from me, for I am gentle

and lowly in heart, and you will find rest for your souls. 13 For my yoke is easy, and my burden is light.

As I was leaving the gym, I noticed a young man entering the gym who looked like he had the weight of the world on his shoulders. He looked worn out, energy spent, and fed up with all the mayhem that was happening throughout the world at this time. The burden of Sisyphus was etched on his face and expressed by his body language as he rolled his boulder up a hill only for it to roll back down upon his troubled life. The irony was not lost on me, in that he would be lifting weights during his workout. I hoped there would be a release during his exercise for his weary soul because at least he was in control of the weight size he would be lifting.

I realized he looked like so many young people who are being crushed under the weight of society's expectations that have been placed on their shoulders. The constant advertising and flash points of mundane information that are consuming the time and peace of everyone who is logged into the world's ever-increasing offerings are draining the resolve of mankind. The accumulated debts of numerous choices to buy everything and anything that would bring meaning to life and comfort for existence, have backfired to the point that no meaning of life has been found and no comfort is attainable. Prov. 23:34 **And you will be as unsteady as one who lies down in the middle of the sea, and as vulnerable to disaster as one who lies down on the top of a ship's mast, saying, 35 "They struck me, but I was not hurt! They beat me, but I did not feel it! When will I wake up? I will seek more wine."**

It does not take many problems before we can find ourselves under the weight of the world. No matter the number of years we have walked with the Lord, we need to daily come to Jesus to find the strength for the day. The apostles who had walked with Jesus for three years should have had a heads-up understanding or had some inside-track information as to how to keep their peace and belief intact when a crisis came along. However, they found themselves under the weight of the world when Jesus was crucified and laid to rest in a tomb behind a massive boulder. When the events Jesus had foretold did happen, the followers of Jesus were fumbling and uncertain of what to do. They had forgotten the lessons Jesus had brought to their souls. Luke 24:6 **He is not here; he has risen! Remember how he told you, while he was still with you in Galilee: 7 'The Son of Man must be delivered over to the hands of sinners, be crucified and on the third day be raised again.'"**

The weight of the world had come upon those who had believed in Jesus but were now shaken in their faith. Luke 24:17 **And He said to them, "What is this conversation that you are holding with each other as you walk?" And they stood still, looking sad.** It was only after they had come into the presence of the risen Lord did the joy and strength of the Lord remove the weight of uncertainty and fear from their hearts and souls. Luke 24:32 **They said to each other, "Weren't our hearts burning within us while He was talking with us on the road and explaining the Scriptures to us?"** Yes, it is while Jesus is talking to us, that we get our equilibrium within our faith back on track. Unlike Sisyphus, we who are in Christ victoriously roll the boulder of doubt, fear, and unbelief over the hill to the other side where it rolls and crashes into little pieces that do not come back to crush our lives.

Asaph, the Psalmist, was carrying the weight of the world to the point that he became jealous of those who did not follow the laws of God. He honestly points out his shortcomings when he says in Psalm 73:2 **But as for me, my feet had almost stumbled, my steps had nearly slipped. 3 For I was envious of the arrogant when I saw the prosperity of the wicked**. Asaph laments that nothing is going right, and it is not fair what the righteous have to go through compared to those who are filthy rich, and as well as what the arrogant toward God get away with—it's too hard to carry. Asaph is weighing the plight of the common man to those who have everything, and the injustice is overwhelming to think about. Psalm 73:16 **When I tried to understand all this, it troubled me deeply**. He realizes that if he were to express these thoughts in words, he would ruin a generation of believers who are going through the same battle. Psalm 73:15 **If I had decided to say these things aloud, I would have betrayed your people**.

As Asaph ponders and wrestles with these thoughts, he receives a clear revelation and honest understanding of the truth after spending time in the presence of the Lord. It is only after bringing his burdens to God does the weight of the world lift from his shoulders and soul. Psalm 73:17 **Then I went into your sanctuary, O God, and I finally understood the destiny of the wicked**. The truth of God's Word comes flooding in, washing away the doubt and misleading lies that Asaph was struggling with. His bold proclamation of God being his Lord is the result of spending time in God's presence. Psalm 73:26 **My health may fail, and my spirit may** grow weak, but God remains the strength of my heart; He is mine forever.

As we walk with God, let us remember that it was through Christ and His blood that we were saved and our souls were renewed to everlasting life. From now and throughout eternity, it will always be through the grace of our Lord Jesus that we are His righteousness. When the weight of life tries to attach itself to our souls, it will forever be Jesus we need to bow down to so that our burden is removed. Let us take time to live in the presence of our Lord.

Question:

What weight of the world are you carrying in your soul that you have not handed over to God to heal for you?

I Deserve To Die

Romans 3:10 There is no one righteous, not even one. 11 There is no one who understands; there is no one who seeks God. 12 All have turned away; all alike have become worthless. There is no one who does what is good, not even one.

I was talking with a dear friend who has been wrestling the prince-powers of darkness and resisting their relentless false accusations and belittling contemptible lies saying, "I deserve to die." Without realizing it, I think the devil had given this person under attack a strategy to use, by declaring the same words of the accusation. Instead of accepting the death that the devil intended, take the same words and find deliverance in the Lord's salvation. If you think about it, we all deserve to die, however, we have a Saviour who decided that while we were dead in our trespasses and sins He loved us anyway and died for us. We did nothing to deserve God's grace toward us and yet the death we deserved was placed upon Jesus. He took our place on the cross where we deserved to be and suffered the eternal death that was coming our way and gave us eternal life instead. This miracle would never have happened had we not deserved to die for our sins.

Talk about a reversal of fortunes. Now, my friend who was under attack could say, "Yes, I deserve to die, but Jesus died for me so that I did not need to." All of us were dead in our sins and iniquities but Jesus took all that death and dying and replaced it with life and living. He gave us eternal life through the cross and His blood. 2Cor. 5:21 **God made Him who knew no sin to be sin on our behalf, so that in Him we might become the righteousness of God**. What an amazing Saviour we have, and an incredible love that was extended to anyone who would accept the Lord's living gift of hope. Yes, Lord, I did deserve to die, but You rescued me through Your gift of salvation. Praise the name of Jesus!

Satan has not changed his tactics since the beginning of his fall from grace. He is still trying to convince people that their lives are not worth living and therefore, tries to bully people into destroying themselves or taking no joy in their lives. In truth, it is the devil's life that is worthless and it is he who will eventually be thrown into the eternal lake of fire and death to suffer everything that he has sown throughout his pathetic existence. Satan has always tried killing the Word of God that lives in a Christian's heart. The enemy of our soul is after the Word of God that can destroy the works of darkness. It is the Word of God working in us that the devil is after. Mark 4:15 **Some are like the word sown on the path. When they hear, immediately Satan comes and takes away the word sown in them.** The Word of the Lord had the power to throw Satan out of heaven; that same powerful Word is in our hearts and has the same authority. This is why he tries to stop God's Word from taking root in a believer's heart.

There is nothing more miraculous than someone who had been walking in darkness and then finding their way into the loving presence of Jesus. How many times has Satan been burned as he watched someone who was walking the paths of sin and death turn their lives around and become alive in Christ? The attacks and malicious plans of the enemy toward the human race are a daily battle for those who are in Christ. The only way to remain on top of the circumstances of life is through the power and blood of our Saviour. Rev. 12:11 **They have conquered him by the blood of the Lamb and by the word of their testimony. And they did not love their lives so as to shy away from death.** Someone might ask if positive thinking can overcome the negatives we come across in life. Yes, we can overcome a lot of problems by being positive. However, if we want to destroy the works of the evil one, we will need the full power of the Holy Spirit and His life-giving Word.

It is the living Word of God who breaks through the maze of confused sinfulness and rescues our souls from destruction. John 1:14 **The Word became flesh** and dwelt among us. **We observed his glory, the glory as the one and only Son from the Father, full of grace and truth**. The Word of God declares Satan's intentions towards all humankind are death, hatred, and destruction. The Lord's will is for salvation, life, and victory. John 10:10 **The thief does not come except to steal, and to kill, and to destroy. I have come that they may have life, and that they may have it more abundantly**. There are two opposites vying for our attention. Whoever we give our minds and hearts to, will rule our souls. Therefore, choose wisely whom you will serve. Satan hates us to death and claims that we deserve to die, while Jesus is Lord, and He loves us with truth and grace. As for me, I will walk with the Lord.

Question:

Have you accepted your gift of righteousness through Christ that God has given you, or are you struggling in believing that you are the righteousness of God through Jesus?

Imprisoned In Circumstances

Deuteronomy 30:19 I call heaven and earth to witness against you today, that I have set before you life and death, blessing and curse. Therefore choose life, that you and your offspring may live.

Everyone has circumstances in their lives that need to be addressed, but we need to choose God's living answers to overcome those circumstances that we have fallen into. Wisdom dictates that we apply and use the Word of God to find our victory and choose God's healing Word for our soul's restoration as we fight the good fight of faith. Deut.30:19 **I call heaven and earth to witness against you today, that I have set before you life and death, blessing and curse. Therefore choose life, that you and your offspring may live**. The battle for life and the right choices to be made throughout our lives will never stop on this side of eternity. We intentionally need to choose God every day.

Life's events can catch a person off guard and in some cases, the unanticipated hardship can devastate a person within a brief moment. As they try to pick themselves off the floor, they find themselves crushed under the circumstances. One day, a person is living what they think is a well-adjusted life, and the next day, all hell has broken loose against them. "What did I do to deserve this?" is the question on the mind of the victim. The answer is simple. We have an eternal enemy and we had better be battle-ready and battle-proven to take on these prince-powers with the weapons our Heavenly Father has given us to defeat all evil. John 10:10a **The thief comes only to steal and kill and destroy**. Otherwise, we will be imprisoned by circumstances, sitting in the dark, wondering what happened to cause such a catastrophic change in our lives. Of course, the enemy of our soul will have all kinds of accusatory reasons for our predicament, but in most cases, the problems that afflicted us showed up because we were not diligent in living God's Word.

The Lord's warnings may have been all around us when we started putting God on the shelf, and not taking time to pray, listen, and reason with Him through His Word. Within a short time, we started drifting back to some of the destructive habits the Lord had previously delivered us from. Then we started ignoring the red flags of danger God was waving at us, as He tried to get our attention. 1Kings 19:11b **Then a great and powerful wind tore the mountains apart and shattered the rocks before the LORD, but the LORD was not in the wind. After the wind there was an earthquake, but the LORD was not in the earthquake. 12 After the earthquake came a fire, but the LORD was not in the fire. And after the fire came a gentle whisper. 13 When Elijah heard it, he pulled his cloak over his face and went out and stood at the mouth of the cave. Then a voice said to him, "What are you doing here, Elijah?"** Yes, a good question. What are we doing here imprisoned in the circumstances of our own doing?

Like Elijah, in the middle of a life storm, we find ourselves looking for God in all the secular places and our perturbation grows into a full anxiety attack of self-condemnation and hate. Meanwhile, God is talking to us in His still small voice expressing His love for us, but we are too caught up in our circumstances to notice. No wonder God says to be still and know that God is God, and we are not. Psalm 46:10a **He says, "Be still, and know that I am God.**

My friend Carolyn testifies to the fact that the more she disciplines herself in following God's Word and taking the time to be with her Lord, she finds her ability to make better life choices has increased a hundredfold. She has noticed that she becomes more productive and fulfilled throughout her days. Carolyn says the correlations are amazing, in that to the degree of time committed to being with Christ and walking in relationship with Him, the results in productivity excel beyond her human ability. By taking the time to be still and know that Jesus is the Lord of all, He gives her the peaceful resolve to do all her work and do it well. Eph. 3:20 **Now to him who is able to do immeasurably more than all we ask or imagine, according to his power that is at work within us.**

Through faith in Christ, the circumstances of life become manageable and even conquerable when we put God first in our lives. Matt. 6:33 **But seek first his kingdom and his righteousness, and all these things will be given to you as well.** When we choose life and allow the Holy Spirit to lead us by His Word, then truly, His Word does become a lamp for the steps we must take in life, and His Word does light up the path we are to walk on. Psalm 119:105 **Your word is a lamp for my feet, a light on my path.** We can break free from the prison of circumstances and become Christians of valour who will become tested and approved in Christ. God commands us to choose life and to live that life to the best of our heart's ability. Therefore, choose life.

Question:

Are you stuck in the same cycle of behaviour or have you found a way to break through with the help of the Lord?

We Are Still That Evil

Genesis 6:5 The LORD saw how great the wickedness of the human race had become on the earth, and that every inclination of the thoughts of the human heart was only evil all the time. 6 So the LORD was sorry he had ever made them and put them on the earth. It broke his heart.

This verse breaks my heart every time I read it. Gen. 6:6 **So the LORD was sorry he had ever made them and put them on the earth. It broke his heart.** I find myself apologizing to God for the wretchedness of mankind, and for the fact that man can be counted on to not be counted on. Imagine God sitting back and saying, "I wish I had never made them." What an indictment against our good intentions, as the result of everything we do, is evil continually. Yes, I'm sure there are a few things we do that come from a well-intentioned heart, but when the heart is corrupted, even what we think might be good and acceptable to God, ends up short of the holy mark. Jer. 17:9 **The human heart is the most deceitful of all things, and desperately wicked. Who really knows how bad it is?**

Those who say we have come a long way to being an enlightened civilization and have made great strides toward moral excellence are fooling themselves. If anything, the rise of the world idiocracy has pointed out that humanity has become anything but enlightened. We continue to hate each other, declare war on one another, and continue to murder those who bring the smallest offence that is contrary to one's beliefs. Gen.

4:23 Lamech said to his wives, "Adah and Zillah, Hear my voice; you wives of Lamech, listen to what I say; for I have killed a man merely for wounding me, and a boy only for striking (bruising) me.

Mankind continues to slip downward toward his base nature of compromise, selfishness, and evil intent. Humanity is no longer looking for the truth, but rather is looking for those who will agree with their views of whatever nonsense they choose to be their truth. 2Tim. 4:3 **For a time is coming when people will no longer listen to sound and wholesome teaching. They will follow their own desires and will look for teachers who will tell them whatever their itching ears want to hear.** When we, the human race, are left to our interpretation of what is right and wrong, we inevitably ruin everything. Without the guiding love, understanding, and instruction of God, we are truly doomed to repeat the evil that took place before Noah's flood when evil was the only thought emanating from a person's heart.

History demonstrates that when mankind reaches a state of perpetual wickedness, becoming doomed is the inevitable result. Eze. 7:7a **Your doom has come to you, O inhabitant of the land. The time has come; the day is near, a day of tumult.** The destruction that mankind brings upon itself also feeds on itself and creates even more disaster. Then the populace looks to their leaders for answers, but the leaders have lost their ability to reason because, in a lot of cases, it was their leadership that led the masses astray. Eze. 7:26 **Calamity upon calamity will come, and rumor upon rumor. They will go searching for a vision from the prophet, priestly instruction in the law will cease, the counsel of the elders will come to an end.** What this so-called enlightened generation seems to forget, is that the wages of sins and the works of iniquity are still death.

As I look around this world that I am part of and see the problems that arise in every part of it, I can understand the need for a Saviour. I, like so many of you, can feel overwhelmed by the chaos that is pouring forth from every corner and field of our planet. We need deliverance from ourselves. The world is truly groaning under the weight of mankind's sins. The very ground became cursed after Adam sinned. How much more is the ground rebelling against the world's perpetual sinfulness? This train of thought can be wearisome. Psalm 73:16 **When I tried to understand all this, it troubled me deeply**. We need to cling to the fact that even though God said He wished He had not created us, He still came in His love for us and delivered our souls from eternal loss through His gift of redemption.

Even though mankind is still as evil as evil can be, the Lord's sacrificial death on the cross for our sake is the olive branch God is extending to us. When He said that we would be in this world but not of this world, God knew what we would be up against throughout our lives. He also knew that everything we would ever need for victory would be found in, lived by, and acquired through the blood of Jesus, who cleanses us from all sins. God's plan for our deliverance in Christ would bring this world into reconciliation by entering the covenant God made for us by accepting His eternal gift. Although everything seems like it is going through constant disaster and destruction, we have a Lord who will guide us through all the mayhem. He will even guide us through the death process. Psalm 48:14 **For this is God, our God for ever and ever; He will be our guide even to death**.

If our Heavenly Father is going to lead us through the uncertainties of dying, we can rest in the fact that God will lead us through life. Go forth, and live to the fullest by being a blessing in this noisy world.

Question:

In light of the evil in this world, what can you do to make life better for all?

As Selfish As Everyone Else

Genesis 4:7 If you do well, will you not be accepted? And if you do not do well, sin is crouching at the door. Its desire is contrary to you, but you must rule over it."

The rude awakening that sometimes hits our hearts and lets us know that we are as selfish as everyone else, can be a stunning blow to our ego. We think we have our souls under control until an opportunity for a test of our free will presents itself. Self-righteousness and self-dependence can cause us to let our guard down, and only after we fail, do we realize how deceived we were. King David was described as a man after God's heart, yet he was as selfish as anyone else who wanted another man's wife. 2Sam. 11:2 **And it came to pass at eventide, that David arose from off his bed, and walked upon the roof of the king's house: and from the roof, he saw a woman bathing; and the woman** was very beautiful to look upon. 4a **David sent some messengers to get her. She came to him and he had sexual relations with her.**

The fact is, King David was selfish and manipulative to the point of conspiring to murder Bathsheba's husband. This is selfishness out of control. David had become utterly consumed with a fierce cyclone of selfishness that was spinning around his heart. Only after he had been confronted by Nathan the prophet concerning his grievous sin did he, after repenting, get his mind and heart back on track with what God had envisioned for him. It does not matter how many years a person has been proclaiming to be a Christian. The opportunity to fall is always at the doorstep of our hearts. Gen. 4:7 **And if you do not do well, sin is crouching at the door. Its desire is contrary to you, but you must rule over it."** At any point, we can stop the madness and repent of the sin that is contaminating our souls, but how difficult that is when the momentum of sin has taken control of the heart.

We all need to mature in God's grace, but as the saying goes, *The gospel is free, but maturity is expensive.* It is necessary to pay the price of maturity regardless of where we need to mature within our lives. The interesting fact about maturity is that when we reach a certain level of maturation, we realize very quickly there is so much more growing to do. On this side of eternity, we will forever need to press into the presence of God so that His light shines on our self-will and anything else that needs repenting of. The glorious light of God's love will guide us into the maturity of becoming strong in character. Isa. 60:1 **Arise, shine, for your light has come, and the glory of the LORD has risen upon you.**

We read the account of a tax collector named Zacchaeus who had seen and felt the blunt end of everyone's selfishness. He saw the character of man in its base form. He would have heard every excuse, from not having the tax money to being blamed for all the abuse the Roman Empire was dishing out. Zacchaeus took part in the graft and subterfuge that tax money by its nature causes. The flow of tax money presents opportunities to be stolen and redirected to many corrupt open palms. He would have seen avaricious souls scratching and clawing for more and more because he was the go-to guy in the tax collection world. It doesn't matter if you are rich or poor, being greedy is available to anyone.

The event that changed Zacchaeus' heart was his divine appointment in the presence of Jesus who acknowledged him as more than just a tax collector. Jesus had called him a son of Abraham. Luke 19:9 **And Jesus said to him, "Today salvation has come to this house, since he also is a son of Abraham**. The Lord brought out in Zacchaeus a maturity that was greater than his selfishness of heart. Luke 19:8 **But Zacchaeus stood up and said to the Lord, "Look, Lord! Here and now I give half of my possessions to the poor, and if I have cheated anybody out of anything, I will pay back four times the amount."** True repentance had come forth from Zacchaeus who had seen and lived the nature of cupidity.

What was the difference between Zacchaeus and Judas Iscariot? Before they encountered Jesus, they were both selfish people, but Zacchaeus received the invitation to mature that comes through repentance when Jesus lavished His love on him. Judas, on the other hand, remained a selfish thief and manipulator, even though he was with Jesus day after day. 2Tim. 3:7 **Ever learning, and never attaining to the knowledge of the truth.** Judas never acknowledged his need to mature in the faith that Jesus was proclaiming, nor did he pay the price of personal sacrifice that is often needed to mature. Therefore, Judas remained as selfish as everyone else.

What has the Lord been speaking to your heart about that can place you precariously near the edge of sin? What laws of the Thou Shall Not variety are you struggling with and causing the joy of the Lord to wane in your life? We can remain as selfish as everyone else or we can grow up and put in the costly heartfelt effort that is truly of the heart and not a ritualistic activity that is a humanistic shadow of God's perfection. The Lord is rarely impressed with half-heartedness. This is why He wants us hot and on fire for the things of God because God's fire cleanses us from all pretence and the dross of manmade religiosity. Only Jesus can cleanse us so that we can wear the robe of righteousness in our Heavenly Father's kingdom. Yes, *The gospel is free, but maturity is expensive.*

Question:

What selfish part of your life do you want to change?

Norm-Isms

If I lie to you, I am a liar; if I lie to myself, I am a fool.

When you are solipsistic, everything is out of orbit.

Be the neighbour you want to have.

Part Two
Believing Within God's Purposes

Working through the unbelief that sometimes occurs in our hearts can be a difficult battle zone to win in. However, through Christ our Saviour, we can do all the things required to fight the good fight of faith, conquer the onslaughts of the enemy, and win the battle challenges we face in our daily walk in the favour of the Lord. Phil. 4:13 **I can do all things through Christ which strengtheneth me.** *As we find our place and purpose in God, we can be assured that our battle was won for us at the cross. Jesus took upon Himself our sins and iniquities so that we would step forward and learn how to be victorious in Him who first loved us. Let us pick up our cross and live in the righteousness that Jesus won for us. 2Cor. 5:21* **For He made Him who knew no sin to be sin for us, that we might become the righteousness of God in Him.**

Religious Competition

2Corinthians 10:12 For we dare not value or compare ourselves against those who flaunt themselves, for those among them who compare themselves are not wise.

The Sermon on the Mount expressly addresses the ways humanity can and does corrupt religion. Jesus points out the importance of keeping our relationship with God intimately personal. Not to turn our relationship with the Almighty into a religious competition for worldwide viewing and bragging rights of self-righteousness. Matt. 5:20 **But I warn you—unless your righteousness is better than the righteousness of the teachers of religious law and the Pharisees, you will never enter the Kingdom of Heaven!** Jesus was saying, "Don't be like the hypocrites or the scribes and Pharisees who make a point of their whole religious existence as something to impress and be seen by the public. Stop trying to out-righteous one another with open exhibitions of ritual activities that have no bearing on what God calls righteousness."

Matthew chapter 23 is an account of Jesus exposing the hypocrisies of the Pharisees, Scribes, Herodians, Sadducees and religious leaders who were taking part in and practising religious zeal. The act of serving God had become a competition of who could out-righteous who on the big stage of godliness. The Lord shows us that this misguided zeal is not of God. This demonstration of self-righteousness creates arguments and bitterness which eventually develops into an us and them social order. Luke 18:10 **Two men went up to the temple to pray, one a Pharisee and the other a tax collector. 11 The Pharisee was standing and praying like this about himself: 'God, I thank you that I'm not like other people—greedy, unrighteous, adulterers, or even like this tax collector.** In this case, the "them" was the tax collector.

History demonstrates that the wars that have been fought over religion have been nonstop since the beginning of time. I'm not going to take time to talk about the Crusades, the Inquisition, or the Holocaust, but in my lifetime the Communist Red Guards persecuted many

Christians and destroyed churches in the late 1950s. We also had the Catholics and the Protestants blowing each other up in the early 1970s to the 1990s in Northern Ireland. We quaintly call that period of religious history *The Troubles*. Within the last few years, many of the Muslim nations have been at odds with the rest of the world and the conflict for religious supremacy is killing thousands. The casualties in all this warfare are the children, the elderly, and civilians who want peace in their lifetime. No one is winning the religious competitions because it is not what God wants of us.

James points out what pure religion is. This might be the place to start exercising what God wants. James 1:27 **Religion that God our Father accepts as pure and faultless is this: to look after orphans and widows in their distress and to keep oneself from being polluted by the world**. In another verse, God says this is the thing to do. Micah 6:8 **He has told you, O man, what is good; and what does the LORD require of you but to do justice, and to love kindness, and to walk humbly with your God?** There is a lot of elbow room in this area of service in God's Kingdom. Not many are jostling to be first up in taking care, being kind, and walking humbly toward orphans and widows while staying unpolluted by the world. The Lord wants us to have a relationship with Him so that we have an understanding of how to love each other. Only in Christ can this miracle take place, otherwise, religion on its own becomes an arena of competition.

When we walk circumspectly before our God and hear His voice leading us, we will not have time to compare ourselves with others and get involved with the religious competitions of the day. 2Cor. 10:12 **For** we dare not value or compare ourselves against those who flaunt themselves, for those among them who compare themselves are not wise. When we are together in eternity, I don't think we will be trying to outshine each other with the rewards God gave us. I am sure we will be genuinely full of joy toward each other for the reason that through Christ we were all redeemed and found our way home. The love that we will express for God and our fellow man will all be because of the sacrifice that Jesus gave of Himself and not the religion we practice on earth. If this is going to be the eternal outcome, then why not put away the limitations we create through our fears? Let us love one another now as the Holy Spirit leads. We need not compete with each other for the love of God, We already have it.

Questions:

Do you find yourself questioning why you take part in certain practices within the structure of your Christianity?

_____

Are you willing to change your ways of doing things in the body of Christ when the Lord points out what needs changing?

_____

Hear The Prophetic Voice

2Chronicles 20:20 And they rose early in the morning, and went forth into the wilderness of Tekoa: and as they went forth, Jehoshaphat stood and said, Hear me, O Judah, and ye inhabitants of Jerusalem: believe in Jehovah your God, so shall ye be established; believe his prophets, so shall ye prosper.

The prophetic voice and vision that the prophet brought forth as a spokesman for God, was taken seriously when destruction was about to take place within a nation. Life and death were dependent upon following the instructions of the prophet who had inquired of God. The Lord's clear directions came down to deliver some and destroy others. Hopefully, those needing God's help were delivered of the calamity surrounding them. God rarely, if ever did anything among His people without first revealing His plans to the prophet. Amos 3:7 **Surely the Lord GOD does nothing without revealing His plan to His servants the prophets**. God gives revelation knowledge and instructions to the prophet, and the prophet in turn gives the people warnings, instructions, and admonitions. With this method of interaction, Almighty God could meet the people's needs and direct their lives in the will of God.

We can see this ordered relationship taking place when God is going to destroy Sodom and Gomorrah. Gen. 18:17 **Then the LORD said, "Shall I hide from Abraham what I am about to do?** The judgment that is planned for Sodom and Gomorrah is explained to

Abraham and Abraham begins to reason with God as to whether destroying the righteous along with the sinful population was the right thing to do. Sadly the only righteous found in the city was Lot, and by default his family. The conclusion that this interaction with Abraham leaves with us demonstrates that had there been a few righteous souls in these two locations, God would have had mercy and spared them. Gen. 18:20 **And the LORD said, Because the cry of Sodom and Gomorrah is great, and because their sin is very grievous.**

The prophet's word was not always welcomed. The people did not always appreciate nor want to believe the prophetic Word of God when the prophet expounded upon God's warnings. King Zedekiah wanted Jeremiah to prophecy nice and favourable outcomes for himself and the lives of the Judeans. As if God was subject to the prophet. Jeremiah ended up incarcerated because he was obeying God and telling the king and the people exactly what God said was going to happen. Jer. 32:3 **Now Zedekiah king of Judah had imprisoned him there, saying, "Why do you prophesy as you do? You say, 'This is what the LORD says: I am about to give this city into the hands of the king of Babylon, and he will capture it. 4 Zedekiah king of Judah will not escape the Babylonians but will certainly be given into the hands of the king of Babylon, and will speak with him face to face and see him with his own eyes.** This was not uncommon for the people to take their anger toward the Lord and lash out at the prophet conveying God's testament.

A surprising amount of people do not like it when the word of a prophetic utterance brings convicting truth to a heart. The result of this word can hurt immensely when a person's heart is set on a particular path or desire and God brings a different instruction for them to follow in their life. We should be grateful that God is directing our lives for our good, but it is still our choice whether we will despise or obey the word. The prophetic instruction is not always comfortable to obey, but it is needed if we are going to grow in the maturity of our faith. 1Thes. 5:20 **Do not treat prophecies with contempt, 21 but test everything that is said. Hold on to what is good.**

We who live in the dispensation of the New Testament, have received through our new birth in Christ, the prophetic abilities of Jesus. Those who have accepted Jesus as Lord, have received Christ's prophetic gifts that live and can be discerned within our souls. It may not always seem apparent because we are seeing through a dark lens, as the Apostle Paul describes it, but nonetheless, we still have the light and insight of the Holy Spirit's prophetic understanding available to us. I believe this is why we are admonished to covet the gift of prophecy. We can prophesy words that bring healing and uplift the spirit within the hearts of mankind 1Cor. 14:1 **Pursue love, and earnestly desire the spiritual gifts, especially that you may prophesy.**

When Jesus ministered as a prophet, He brought life and direction. John 1:48 **Nathanael said to Him, "How do You know me?" Jesus answered and said to him, "Before Philip called you, when you were under the fig tree, I saw you."** Jesus ministered to people's hearts by bringing a prophetic insight into the depths of a person's soul. He could touch the spot within a heart that when healed their lives would be changed. This was the case with the Samaritan woman Jesus met at the well. She was looking for fulfilment through the men she had lived with but found no solution to her deep longings. However, just one encounter with the Lord's loving grace and He met her need. John 4:18 **The fact is, you have had five husbands, and the man you now have is not your husband. What you have just said is quite true**. The prophetic insight hit her heart. John 4:19 **The woman saith unto him, Sir, I perceive that thou art a prophet.** Not only was her life changed but the people of the town were also changed. John 4:40 **So when the Samaritans came to him, they urged him to stay with them, and he stayed two days.** This one prophetic word in season brought about a two-day revival of faith in God. John 4:41 **And because of his words many more became believers.**

Jesus foretold the fall and destruction of the temple. Mark 13;2 **And Jesus said to him, "Do you see these great buildings? There will not be left here one stone upon another that will not be thrown down."** According to the historian Josephus, the temple was captured and destroyed a generation later. Jesus used His gift of prophecy as well as His office of a prophet. We need to discern between the office of a prophet and the gift of prophecy. Just because I have a few prophetic insights into what the Lord is teaching me on a particular subject, does not mean I have been called to the office of a prophet over a nation, state or country. The gift of prophecy is for all believers in Christ. Because of our salvation through Christ, we must protect the prophetic voice of the Spirit that arises within us. This puts a whole new seriousness on the words we speak to ourselves and each other. May we covet the gift of prophecy and may we use this gift to wash one another in the healing words of the Lord.

Question:

Do you know the difference between the gift of prophecy and the office of a Prophet?

Status Confessionis

Acts 4:11 This Jesus is 'the stone that was rejected by you, the builders; it has become the cornerstone.' 12 And there is salvation in no one else; for there is no other name under heaven that has been given among people by which we must be saved for God has provided the world no alternative for salvation."

Status confessionis means that a particular doctrine is essential to who we are as a church. If something is status confessionis it means this is a make or break issue.

There are a lot of issues in the church that many people argue about and even become angrily embittered to the point of leaving the church assembly they were attending. Many of the issues of controversy are over traditions that have been implemented by different denominational groups with varying beliefs and methods of expressing worship, praise, and love for God. I can normally let most of these disagreements slide by because the Word of God instructs us not to argue about words, just for the sake of arguing. 2Tim. 2:14 **Remind the people of these facts, and solemnly charge them in the presence of God to avoid petty controversy over words, which does no good, and**

upsets and undermines and ruins the faith of those who listen. However, as for the foundation of my heart's eternal hope and belief, my make-or-break issue is my unwavering faith in that Jesus Christ is Lord and the only way of salvation.

Jesus Christ is the only Saviour of the world, and this may be the status confessionis of our time. This foundational belief of faith in God and His intervention on man's behalf to reconcile our lives to Himself on His terms is the gift of salvation we can trust in. Jesus said He is the only way to our heavenly Father, and no one can come to God the Father except through Jesus Christ. John 14:6 **Jesus said to him, "I am the way, and the truth, and the life. No one comes to the Father except through me.** I believe there are many roads to Jesus as so many testimonies can attest to that fact, but there is only one way to God the Father. The only acceptable sacrifice that God would accept to wash away the sins of the world was the sacrifice of His Son, and with the blood of Jesus that was spilled on the torturous cross.

Jesus did not come to make bad people good, He came to make dead people live. Our Lord did not come to make Christians follow Christianity, He came to lead us in following Christ. The Lord did not come to give us a united cause, He came to unite us in the love He has for us. Rom. 5:8 **But God proves His love for us in this: While we were still sinners, Christ died for us.** Jesus did not come so that we might all get along, He came so that we would love one another as Christ loves us. 1John 4:19 **We love because He first loved us.** Our Lord did not come to teach us social etiquette, He came to teach us the Gospel of Jesus Christ who takes away the sins of the world.

61

The Lord asked Peter and the disciples "Who do the crowds and people say I am?" Peter answers similarly to what people are saying today. "Well Lord, they say you are a teacher, a good man with a prophetic gift. Some are saying you are a mystic healer." Matt. 16:14 **And they said, "Some say John the Baptist, others say Elijah, and others Jeremiah or one of the prophets."** The Lord asks Peter and the disciples the key question. Matt. 16:15 **He said to them, "But who do you say that I am?"** 16 **Simon Peter replied, "You are the Christ, the Son of the living God."** This is the crux of our very existence in the faith. Who do we say Jesus is? Is He the Saviour or not? Today there is a smorgasbord of answers as to who Jesus is, and some are questioning the existence of the historic Jesus let alone the risen Lord.

Like the Apostle Paul, we need to be in Christ and be without doubt that Jesus is Lord and the only eternal answer whom God the Father has given to mankind as a gift and way to eternal life. Phil. 1:21 **For to me, to live is Christ He is my source of joy, my reason to live and to die is gain for I will be with Him in eternity.** There is no salvation in any other. We are warned that in the last days, there will be a great falling away from the faith and fickleness will be the choice over reason. 2Tim. 4:3 **For the time will come when people will not tolerate sound doctrine and accurate instruction that challenges them with God's truth; but wanting to have their ears tickled with something pleasing, they will accumulate for themselves many teachers one after another, chosen to satisfy their own desires and to support the errors they hold.**

There is nothing new here. We still have the choice to eat from one of the two trees in the Garden of Eden.

We can eat from the tree of knowledge of good and evil, where we can be like God and make our own choices as to who and what we want enthroned upon our hearts. As Satan said, "We will be like God, intimately knowing good and evil." But multiple times better, we can eat from the Tree of Life which is Christ the Lord. We can choose to eat and live upon every Word of loving grace that God the Father lavishes on us. We can walk in the salvation that the Lord has freely provided for us all. What an amazing sacrifice of love we have been given. Jesus my Lord, who first loved me, is my status confessionis.

Question:

Do you believe that if we do not get the Lordship of Jesus established in our hearts, we will not get the understanding of our life purpose resolved in our hearts?

Conspirituality

Isaiah 8:12 "Do not call conspiracy everything this people calls a conspiracy; do not fear what they fear, and do not dread it.

In the book *Conspirituality* by Derek Beres, he describes the overlap of conspiracy theories with spirituality, typically of New Age varieties. The author describes the follies, frauds, cons and cults that dominate the New Age and wellness industries, and how they betray the trust of people.

What I have noticed about all these new age movements and imitation spiritual lifestyles, is that there is nothing new under the sun. Eccl. 1:9 **What has been will be again, what has been done will be done again; there is nothing new under the sun.** These alternatives or feigned enlightened teachings have been around since the construction of the Tower of Babel was interrupted by God Himself. The alarming part of these alternative movements is how much of this overlapping conspirituality is showing up in the church. If the devotees of these psychological followings would put the same amount of time and study into the Word of God, and take the time to immerse themselves in the Lord's presence, they would become spiritually mature people and able to understand the Word of truth and know when they are being duped. Eph. 4:14 **Then we will no longer be infants, tossed about by the waves and carried around by every wind of teaching and by the clever cunning of men in their deceitful scheming.**

The Lord wants us to learn and ask Him the hard questions and to discover the ever-increasing faith that is available to us through Christ our only Saviour. God says that it is honourable for us to seek out a Godly mystery that He presents to us. Prov. 25:2 **It is the glory of God to conceal a thing, but the honour of kings is to search out a matter.** In the book of Revelation Chapter One Verse Six, the Word of God says that we are kings and priests unto God. Therefore, we have God's permission to find out whether or not the spiritual mystery we are getting involved with will bring life or destruction to our faith.

There is an issue when people become involved in a conspiracy or an alternative religious obsession. They do not discern their beliefs wisely, and begin declaring anything said by anyone that does not agree with their newfound views as a conspiracy against themselves. They take the disagreement of belief as an attack against their very existence. At this point, their deception deepens to where they are now alienating family and friends because they are offended at anyone bringing forth an opposing view. Isa. 8:12**"Do not call conspiracy everything this people calls a conspiracy; do not fear what they fear, and do not dread it.** For those whose lives are captured by dark conspiracies or cults, the cult often separates people from the ones who love them, and no amount of reasoning will work until the spiritual power promoting the cult is broken.

The Word of God is continually reminding us to stay vigilant and aware that the enemy of our soul is out to corrupt the hearts of all humanity and to desecrate the Word of God. This is why we are admonished to study God's Word and to apply it to our lives with God's grace. 2Tim. 2:15 **Be diligent to present yourself approved to God, a worker who does not need to be ashamed, rightly dividing the word of truth.** Furthermore, we are instructed to test the spirits that bring forth questionable doctrines. 1John 4:1 **Dear friends, do not believe everyone who claims to speak by the Spirit. You must test them to see if the spirit they have comes from God. For there are many false prophets in the world.** When new ideologies come to us and these beliefs do not acknowledge Jesus Christ is Lord, then rebuke that spirit and move on. Take a big imaginary stamp that says *Return To Sender,* stamp that false doctrine with it, and send it back to hell from whence it came.

The Apostle Paul emphasized that if an angel should appear teaching an anti-Christ doctrine, then that angel is to be rebuked as well. Gal. 1:8 **But even if we or an angel out of heaven should preach a gospel to you contrary to what we proclaimed to you, let him be accursed!** It seems to me that the number of warnings we get through God's Word to be on guard for false teachings and to be swift to remove them from our conscience as soon as the erroneous teaching is noticed means that heresy is still a problem in our time. I do not know if the word *conspirituality* will become a buzzword, but it does describe the homogenization of a worldwide religion that seems hell-bent on taking the Lord's place on the altar of our hearts.

The question becomes, what are we to do with the smorgasbord of spiritual options that are out there? As I grow older and become mature in my faith, I have noticed that obeying the Word of God is not a complicated process. The Apostle James says to be a doer of the Word and not a hearer only. He writes, in James 1:25 **But whoever looks intently into the perfect law that gives freedom, and continues in it—not forgetting what they have heard, but doing it—they will be blessed in what they do**. As Christians, we are to line up what we read and learn with the instructions God gives us in His Word. Go and do likewise. May the Lord's truth and peace lead us all.

Questions:

Do you find it hard to share your faith in Christ with others?

_____

Do you want to share your faith in Christ with others, and if so what is your strategy?

_____

Missing The Mark

1John 1:9 If we confess our sins, He is faithful and righteous, so that He will forgive us our sins and cleanse us from all unrighteousness.

Sometimes, we miss the mark God has set as His standard for righteousness and walking free of bondage. At some point during our walk of faith with Christ, we will sin. The question is, "What are we going to do when this happens?" The voice of conviction that the Holy Spirit brings to our soul is a message that encourages us to quickly come boldly to the throne of God the Father and repent. Heb. 4:16 **Let us then approach God's throne of grace with confidence, so that we may receive mercy and find grace to help us in our time of need**. When do we need God's mercy and grace? When we sin, and fall flat on our faces. The mercy and grace God has for us will help us confess our sins and we will be washed of our unrighteousness. 1John 1:9 **If** we confess our sins, He is faithful and righteous, so that He will forgive us our sins and cleanse us from all unrighteousness.

Why do some of us keep falling in the same area of sin? Beside the point that sometimes people enjoy the sin they are taking part in, the temptation of sin will keep coming back because the enemy of our soul knows that some temptations work when we are in a vulnerable state within our hearts and minds. It says in the book of Luke that Jesus overcame the temptations in the desert and that Satan would come back and try to tempt Him again when there was more of an opportunity to do so. Luke 4:13 **And when the devil had ended every temptation, he departed from him until an opportune time.** My observation is that if this happened to Jesus, then we can be sure it will happen to us.

Someone might say, "But I have been walking with the Lord for years and I still struggle with this sin." Judas walked, hung out, and was discipled by Jesus for three years, and still fell apart in his soul. Paul and Barnabus taught the deep teachings of the New Testament and had a terrible falling out over an argument about the integrity of Mark. Struggles and temptations will come and keep coming until we have lived and breathed our last breath on this earth. The Apostle Peter had fallen to peer pressure. Paul confronted him because Peter was a pretender who rejected his own principles. Gal. 2:11 **However, when Ce′phas (Peter) came to Antioch, I resisted him face-to-face, because he was clearly in the wrong. 12 For before certain men from James arrived, he used to eat with people of the nations; but when they arrived, he stopped doing this and separated himself, fearing those of the circumcised** class. 13 **The rest of the Jews also joined him in putting on this pretense, so that even Bar′na·bas was led along with them in their pretense. 14 But when I saw that they were not walking in step with the truth of the good news, I said to Ce′phas before them all: "If you, though you are a Jew, live as the nations do and not as Jews do, how can you compel people of the nations to live according to Jewish practice?"**

Not only did Peter's hypocrisy affect the new gentile converts in Christ, but he also had a negative effect on the Jews who also took part in the hypocrisy. Sin begets sin, and righteousness begets righteousness. If these giants in the faith were struggling with the issues of their day, then we need the grace and mercy of our Lord to wash us clean when we repent of our sins. Jealousy, greed, immorality, wrath, blasphemy, theft and murderous thoughts are with us until we leave this earth. We need a Saviour who can keep us from falling and assure us that we will not be lost to the world. The blood of Jesus is the most powerful sin-cleansing gift that God gave us so that we would remain in fellowship with the Lord forever. 2Pet. 3:9 **The Lord is not slow in keeping His promise as some understand slowness, but is patient with you, not wanting anyone to perish but everyone to come to repentance.**

Have you found yourself in a place where you have missed the mark AGAIN? Take heart for the throne of grace is waiting for your visitation. There is a place for you at God's throne to lay your heart down at Jesus' feet. Ask the Lord of mercy to wash you clean and to give you the grace needed to get back up and go forth in the assurance of your salvation. Come and reason with God even though you feel like an unworthy soul. Isa. 1:18 **Come now, let us reason together," says the LORD. "Though your sins are like scarlet, they will be as white as snow; though they are as red as crimson, they will become like wool.** It is up to us to come and repent, and it is the Lord's joy to forgive us. Believe in the saving grace of our Lord for it is life to those who find it.

Question:

What are the most difficult temptations you have had to battle?

Porneia

Proverbs 20:12 The hearing ear, and the seeing eye, the LORD hath made even both of them.

Vincent van Gogh said, "Conscience is a man's compass."

The spirit of porneia. It is one of those topics that can polarize and bring acrimonious debate and that is not my intention. I want people to know that this habit, like any bad habit can be conquered. I will try to establish a starting point for the people and families who are struggling with the consequences and feelings of helplessness that can occur when a pornographic spirit has brought harm to a relationship. I hope this article helps clear up some of the thought processes that will be needed to overcome this vice and any other bondage that has control within a soul.

Part 1: The Eye OF Porneia

It is difficult for people who have tried to stop entertaining themselves with the vice of porneia to admit that there is a stronghold in their lives because there is often harsh treatment that comes from their closest friends and family members when the user is exposed. There is a plague-like attitude that results toward the participants of porneia when they come forth asking for help, guidance, and prayer in the areas of this obsession. Most of the time it is because the people close to the one asking for help have as many hang-ups and secret sins themselves that no one looks for answers because there seems to be no way out. 1Cor. 10:13 **There hath no temptation taken you but such as is common to man: but God is faithful, who will not suffer you to be tempted above that ye are able; but will with the temptation also make a way to escape, that ye may be able to bear it.**

There is a way out, but there has to be a real desire to get out of porneia's grasp. No half-measures work because porneia is like leaven; it affects the whole body, soul, and spirit of a person. Porneia is a spirit that causes multiple hurts within families, marriages, and individuals. My personal belief is that we have been approaching this subject (craving porn), from the point of an addiction rather than an obsession. Addictions have a bodily desire; a craving, such as ingesting drugs, alcohol, cigarette smoke and excessive food eating disorders where the body is addicted to these substances. However, gambling, compulsive spending, kleptomania, hoarding, and participating in the multiple activities of porneia are obsessions. Some might say at this point, "You say potato and I say, blah blah blah."

I am putting forth an observation from when I have helped people overcome their addictions and helped people sort out their obsessions. The approach is different when dealing with an obsession because the obsessed are dealing with a passion for mental titillation rather than a craving of bodily ingesting of an addictive substance. Both are an invasion of the soul and the person who is in bondage with an addiction or obsession just wants to be free of it regardless of the label put on it. Both approaches need the Word of God as the foundational truth and power to overcome when the chronic user is honestly ready to defeat this destructive behavior in their lives. Matt. 6:23 **But if thine eye be evil, thy whole body shall be full of darkness. If therefore the light that is in thee be darkness, how great is that darkness!**

What is the spirit of porneia? Is it only a seductive spirit that saps our spiritual strength or is it just a cheap-thrills activity men and women entertain themselves with? The problem with trying to give a reader's digest version of porneia (a Greek word) that encompasses most sexual sin causes a deluded interpretation of its culpability within the souls of the afflicted. The best we seem to come up with is a quick and substandard answer; so we say, "It means pornography." That is like saying, "Einstein was pretty good at math." There is more to it, but because we do not like to associate with this subject we end up with a diluted answer and a weak battle plan for overcoming it.

This sin, like all other sins, is forgiven when repented of. However, those entangled by its merciless pull have a difficult time accepting the forgiveness offered to them. Why? One of the reasons is that the spouse and family members affected by it, often have an onerous time forgiving the one asking for forgiveness and help. This happens even though God is willing to forgive and has forgiven entirely. Matt.12:31a **Wherefore I say unto you, All manner of sin and blasphemy shall be forgiven unto men**.

We lean toward having a personal measuring stick when it comes to certain types of sin. We tend to borrow a page from the Roman Catholic catechism as in mortal and venial sins. A really big sin is much harder to forgive but a small one, ah, no problem. Sorry, Saints. Sin is sin, and God forgives all manner of sin when repented of—even the big ones. 1John 5:17a **All unrighteousness is sin**. The finished work of the cross has grace for all sin and those who repent of immorality are forgiven.

Will there be some difficulty and challenging choices for the repentant to make as they now live and go forward in a different direction toward victory? Yes, absolutely. Their routines and thought processes will have to be radically acted upon to break away from their seductive worn-out paths that are still clearly etched in their minds. They will need to make difficult choices whether to even log on to a computer or not.

These people will need help fighting their good fight of faith to win their war on porneia, and with the Holy Spirit's leading, it can be done. Rom. 10:17 **So then faith comes by hearing, and hearing by the word of**

God. With deliberate choices and a prayer-led recovery, they can become victors and no longer victims of the obsessive foul spirit of porneia. We all have to remember to keep an eye on our own hearts when discerning the ones going through this battle. Gal. 6:1 **Brethren, if a man be overtaken in a fault, ye which are spiritual, restore such an one in the spirit of meekness; considering thyself, lest thou also be tempted.**

Part 2: The Eye ON Porneia

Philip R. Leineweber says in his thesis, (PORNEIA IN THE MATTHEAN EXCEPTION CLAUSES.) He says, *"The scholarly understanding of the word porneia, it is important to realize that it is broadly used and understood to mean: the general term for all illicit or immoral sexual intercourse. The specific form may sometimes be indicated by the context. If the payment of wages is involved, it is prostitution. If it involves close relatives, it is incest. If it involves persons of the same sex, it is homosexuality. If it involves an unmarried couple, it is unchaste. If it involves a married person outside of marriage, it is adultery."*

As you have just read there is a broad meaning to the word porneia as it crosses a smorgasbord of immoral activity; thus the spirit of porneia is what needs to be defeated. In the Gospel of Matthew, we read an exhortation that if our eye needs discipline then be drastically proactive to defeat whatever vice has captured the eye of our heart. Matt. 5:29 **And if thy right eye offend thee, pluck it out, and cast it from thee: for it is profitable for thee that one of thy members should perish, and not that thy whole body should be cast into hell.**

I am not advocating ripping your eyes out of your head. In context, the Word is saying go the distance to overcome your personal battle. Do whatever it takes to win this demonic attack. For example, I know a man who cancelled all his Internet use at home and kept his iPhone only so he could accommodate his business emails and make his calls. He said that he did not have the fight in him to overcome the pornographic temptation in his home. Some might say, "He is not dealing with the problem, he is just skirting around it." I say, "Good for him." The battle starts and is won with one thought at a time or as the Word of God says, "Line upon line, precept upon precept." His attempt may seem weak in someone's eye but God can take that first step and turn it into a leap of victorious faith. Matt. 12:20 **A bruised reed shall He not break, and smoking flax shall He not quench, till He send forth judgment unto victory. 21 And in His name shall the Gentiles trust.**

The paradox with sexual sin is that sex, in general, is so overrated that it has been made numbingly boring by TV sitcoms. A general blasé attitude and cheap exploitations that cause an emptiness of joy have become a status quo. Prov. 29:3b **But he that keeps company with harlots spends his substance.** On the other hand, sex is so underrated because those who have nurtured and developed a wonderful sex life with their spouse can only thank God for this incredible gift and fulfillment. Gen. 2:25 **And they were both naked, the man and his wife, and were not ashamed.** Prov. 5:18 **Let thy fountain be blessed: and rejoice with the wife of thy youth. 19 Let her be as the loving hind and pleasant roe; let her breasts satisfy thee at all times; and be thou ravished always with her love.**

Another paradox that faces us concerning sex is that unlike an addiction to drug use, where we can eventually stop using the drug, the addiction ends because consumption ends. If someone is obsessed with porn they cannot stop having sex with their spouse, so the problem becomes insidious because it literally follows them into the bedroom. When I was an alcoholic, I prayed and asked God to remove the craving from me and I made sure not to buy any more alcohol or accept it when it was offered. I covenanted that I would not drink anymore. Thank God I was delivered from that addiction and have been sober every day since; therefore, overcoming an addiction by grace. I do not need to bring alcohol with me into the house, bedroom or relationship. The arousal obsession, and excess chronic consumption, affect the binge mechanism with the spirit of porneia. This causes a problem in that porn captivates the soul and mind with thoughts and pictures that have burned themselves into the psyche of the afflicted. Therefore, the spirit of porneia will come with the user into the bedroom during marital relations. The eventual problem will be as the proverb says in Prov. 23:33 **Thine eyes shall behold strange women, and thine heart shall utter perverse thing**.

Therein is the paradox. We can give up drugs and gambling, but we cannot give up intercourse in our marriages as this is convenantly owned between both spouses. This is why the spirit of porneia is at work in great force today. One may be involved with porneia, but two are eventually being scarred and hurt. The enemy of our souls wants to destroy us in every part of our lives and that includes our most intimate moments of marriage as well. John 10:10 **The thief comes not, but** for to steal, and to kill, and to destroy: I am come that they might have life, and that they might have it more abundantly.

With the easy accessibility of porneia from all avenues within our society, there will have to be an honest desire to overcome this spirit that afflicts family life. The first thing that has to be expressed from the heart of the afflicted is to call porneia the evil it is because being lulled into its web has no happy ending. Prov. 9:17 **Stolen waters are sweet, and bread eaten in secret is pleasant.** 18 **But he knows not that the dead are there; and that her guests are in the depths of hell.**

Part 3: The Eye OFF Porneia

In a Pansexual overcharged society, creating real intimate marital memories with our spouse rather than imagining unattainable and unrealistic sexual fantasies with others, is the direction and path needed to look toward. The first step in the battle strategy for overcoming a life controlled by porneia is to first change the thought process by magnifying the solution, and the Lord is the solution. I know this sounds old-fashioned but God is still God and the plan of life that He has established from the beginning is still the right plan. Magnifying Jesus, rather than being led by the overcharged flesh, is the only long-term way out of the stronghold controlling the thoughts of the obsessed. There will have to be some radicalism in the person's life and mind who is fighting this spirit of lust. Learning to say "No" to ourselves may be common sense to some, but it is a new concept to many. Self-denial is not something that is promoted in this over-indulgent time in our history. Consumption is the god of this age.

The morality of many is being challenged with hyper sensations and strong feelings because the obsessed are rationalizing their behavior while walking in their personal version and interpretation of God's Word. They are re-writing the Word of God to suit their cravings. "How far can I go before it becomes sin?" is a question I've been asked. The fact that this question has been asked, means they have gone too far already. James 1:14 **But every man is tempted, when he is drawn away of his own lust, and enticed. 15 Then when lust hath conceived, it brings forth sin: and sin, when it is finished, brings forth death**. I had a Bible study with a young unmarried couple who were asking that very question, "How far can we go?" They did not like my answer when I said, "You have gone too far already." With a few light questions, it was obvious that they had been involved in full marital relations already and their consciences were bothering them both. Thank God there is grace and forgiveness for all our sins and that the young couple's conscience was still being heard.1John 1:9 If **we confess our sins, he is faithful and just to forgive us our sins, and to cleanse us from all unrighteousness**.

Someone said, "The chains of habit are too light to be felt until they're too heavy to be broken." Part of the problem with breaking a habit of any kind is the slothful attitude of "Here God, you take this bad habit from me. Take my cigarettes, Lord!" News flash! God does not smoke so why would He want them? "Make me stop overeating, Lord!" No, you stop the habit of hanging out in the pantry and refrigerator. We want God to take the habit from us with no effort from our hearts to give it up.

There has to be an honest choice and free will that comes from the very core of our being to break any distressing habit. The Word of God says that we are to humble ourselves before God. It is not God who humbles us, but we who humble ourselves. 1Pet. 5:6 **Humble yourselves therefore under the mighty hand of God, that he may exalt you in due time: 7 Casting all your care upon him; for he cares for you.** The Word says to come to Him boldly, not being forced and dragged along. Heb. 4:16 **Let us therefore come boldly unto the throne of grace, that we may obtain mercy, and find grace to help in time of need.**

The desire to overcome sin must come from our honest relationship with God. True, we come to God utterly lost and without hope but we still ask to be saved by the drawing grace of the Holy Spirit. The chronic user of porneia has to choose to make an effort to overcome the obsession they are bound up with because they will never get their fill in the activity, and deep down the one who is hooked knows it. Prov. 27:20 **Hell and destruction are never full; so the eyes of man are never satisfied.** The pornographer will have to make a covenant with his own heart and eyes. Job 31:2 **I made a covenant with mine eyes; why then should I think upon a maid?**

There have been some statistics lately that indicate there has been a drop in Internet porn activity. Statistics are fleeting and can change in a day, but more importantly, there are more sites opening up dedicated to helping anyone who wants to get unhooked from their chronic porn activities. The testimonials from these people who have looked for help and got it are just wonderful to hear. Just after ninety days of porn-free living, they have made great strides toward freedom. Their productivity at work, home, hobbies, and healing in their marriages is a common statement from these former users.

One of the common statements they declare with genuine excitement is that it has been worth the extreme effort they are taking to change their lives. With real joy, they state categorically that the battle is worth it. In most cases, these are people who do not know the Lord and His miraculous power, and these are some of the results as they reach for victory. How much more could be accomplished with God healing the obsessed to victory? Isa. 40:31 **He gives power to the faint; and to them that have no might he increases strength. Even the youths shall faint and be weary, and the young men shall utterly fall: But they that wait upon the LORD shall renew their strength; they shall mount up with wings as eagles; they shall run, and not be weary; and they shall walk, and not faint.**

Part 4: No Eyes FOR Porneia

There is a billboard with a call for help phone number showing up in British Columbia that says, "When gambling is no longer fun." Well, maybe there should be a billboard for the people who are hooked on porneia as well because it can be a wrecking ball to good family life just as much as gambling does its terrible work. As I indicated in the above chapters, everyone gets affected by the people in their lives who are hooked on anything self-destructive.

The spirit of porneia affects all genders, social classes, and nations on this earth. Women are surprised when they hear that other women can be hooked on porn. I am surprised that anyone can be surprised about anything anymore. Eccl. 1:9 **The thing that hath been, it is that which shall be; and that which is done is that which shall be done: and there is no new thing under the sun.**

There is nothing new here as far as vice is concerned. All genders are being tempted by the spirit of porneia and all genders need deliverance. They need to know that there is a way out. Nothing is hopeless when the Lord is on your side, helping you become victorious. What is the reward for the obsessed who have kicked the habit? Happy is the man whose sins are forgiven, yes happy is that man! Psalm 32:2 **Yes, what joy for those whose record the LORD has cleared of guilt, whose lives are lived in complete honesty!**

Learning to say "No" to a bad habit is a new habit that will be established and must first happen in the heart. Jer. 29:13 **And ye shall seek me, and find me, when ye shall search for me with all your heart.** If a person does not have the heart or grit for victory to defeat this obsession, then how can they expect the transformation of the heart? There is no weaning off of an obsession. Cutting that malicious spirit's umbilical cord must be clean and complete. Perhaps borrowing the words of Jesus might become the battle cry that has to be loud and clear when shouted, "It is finished!" Choosing to focus on other things will bring life to the wounded soul. Phil. 4:8 **Finally, brethren, whatsoever things are true, whatsoever things are honest, whatsoever things are just, whatsoever things are pure, whatsoever things are lovely, whatsoever things are of good report; if there be any virtue, and if there be any praise, think on these things.**

When this iniquity is brought to the Lord for healing in the soul and memories, it is not something that is beyond the redemptive work of the cross. This sin and every other conceivable sin have been forgiven by God's redemptive grace. This gift has been offered to anyone who wants their freedom from the bondage of any kind. When sin is repented of, it was not the first time that Jesus heard of it. The Lord carried every thought and sinful activity that ever was, is, and will be on the cross.

The complete accusations of every sin known to man were nailed right in the Lord's flesh to the cross, where the penalty of sin was paid in full. Don't let the enemy of your soul tell you that this particular sin (that is most often done in secret), cannot be forgiven. It has been forgiven openly with the holy blood of Christ and His resurrection power that lives in us all who have received Him as Lord. 1Pet. 1:3 **Blessed be the God and Father of our Lord Jesus Christ, which according to his abundant mercy hath begotten us again unto a lively hope by the resurrection of Jesus Christ from the dead.**

Yes, God made our eyes and they can be used to look at whatever we want. However, if we could use them to see what Jesus sees, then we would be in awe of the love and future God has for us. Eph. 3:20 **Now unto him that is able to do exceeding abundantly above all that we ask or think, according to the power that works in us**. God can and will help anyone bound to overcome anything wicked or evil. He can break the chains of any unwanted bondage, obsession, addiction or ugly habit we may be wallowing in. As we look for our place in the purposes of God, let us, with the Holy Spirit's guidance, break whatever hinders us from finding and fulfilling God's righteous call for our lives. Ask for His help and see what the Lord can do.

Questions:

Are you struggling with an addiction, obsession, or secret habit that is crushing your spirit?

_____

Have you asked God for a plan of attack to overcome what has defeated your attempts to conquer what grieves your heart?

_____

Have you been praying for someone who desperately needs to come out from the sin that so easily besets them?

_____

There are always outliers, but these are observations I have noticed over the years of being in sales. The proverb is true. The borrower is a servant to the lender.

There are always outliers, but these are observations I have noticed over the years of being in sales.

The proverb is true. The borrower is a servant to the lender.

Norm-Isms

Don't go into business with anyone who does not have as much to lose as you do.

Silent partners are the noisiest.

Give your customers more than they asked for, but make sure you charge them for what they asked for.

Going into business on a shoestring budget normally means you will end up selling your shoes to stay in a just-making-it business.

Don't let people without money tell you how to spend your money.

Cultural Pitfalls

Romans 12:2 **Don't copy the behavior and customs of this world, but let God transform you into a new person by changing the way you think. Then you will learn to know God's will for you, which is good and pleasing and perfect.**

Shawn Smucker writes, "As has been the case in far too many instances, Christianity conforms to culture. Christians of every ilk set up idols of particular beliefs, polarizing themselves into camps of Correct and Incorrect."

It is worse than what Shawn says. Cultural defensiveness is often the litmus test as to whether we will believe what is being said about God. Historically, the culture of the day has dictated the Christian's acceptance of political choices, regional beliefs, and the temptations at hand within the era the culture is part of. We have in some cases made the Christian faith no more than a social club to be part of because the people are nice and pleasant to be around. The church will never get permission from the world to bring God's righteous standard to a culture that welcomes vice and iniquity as normal behaviour. The world system is corrupt, and calling something evil as being good, is its default setting. Isa. 5:20 **Woe to those who call evil good and good evil, who turn darkness to light and light to darkness, who replace bitter with sweet and sweet with bitter.**

The amalgamation that the body of Christ and the present-day culture bring together, has hindered the power of the Holy Spirit to move freely within the hearts of believers. Vexing the Holy Spirit with what we deem as culturally acceptable does not bring freedom to our souls because God will resist our acceptance of sin. This attitude has produced an immature Christian who excels in self-righteousness and lives by an insipid doctrine of tolerance toward anything that sounds like a homily. 2Tim. 3:5 **Even though they will make a show of being religious, their religion won't be real. Don't have anything to do with such people**. Do not make holy covenants with people who do not put Jesus first in their hearts.

The Apostle Paul pleaded with the Galatians to rethink their direction and the cultural choices they were making because they were going backwards in their faith. Those who were teaching the erroneous doctrines of salvation by working the laws of self-righteousness were creating a culture that had deceived the Galatians into thinking they could earn a place on God's board of directors (paraphrased), while still living the life of what was socially acceptable. Gal. 3:1 **O foolish Galatians! Who has bewitched you? It was before your eyes that Jesus Christ was publicly portrayed as crucified**. The cultural norms had wormed their way into their hearts and they began accepting philosophies that would distort the simple message of salvation in Christ. Gal. 3:3 **How foolish can you be? After starting your Christian lives in the Spirit, why are you now trying to become perfect by your own human effort?**

What this type of self-righteous dogma does to a soul, is create a survival of the fittest religiosity that results in the cruelties and butchery of the Crusades, or the brutal torture of the Inquisition. It allows carnal choices to be made in the name of God, and within a short period, an idea like the Holocaust becomes a reasonable solution to a certain cultural group. You cannot wash your clothes in filthy water and expect them to come out clean and fresh. Yet this is what mankind does when they compromise their Christian faith so they can be accepted in the culture of the day, or they bring the current culture into their interpretation of which scripture they will accept. Culturally processing their personal salvation plan through all the filth of human philosophy and then wondering why they do not feel clean of heart nor have peace of mind. Gal. 3:1 **Oh, foolish Galatians! Who has cast an evil spell on you? For the meaning of Jesus Christ's death was made as clear to you as if you had seen a picture of his death on the cross.**

Self-righteousness normally creates a maladroit culture that exists just outside the boundaries of God's kingdom. It looks religious, but this existence will not bring anyone into the presence of God. On the contrary, it ensures they continue to flounder in self-deception. It's like the nations who lived around the encampment of Israel and could see the Tabernacle in the wilderness from afar but had no way of entering the protection that God's presence offered those who lived within the camp. The warnings that God gave the Israelites to not be like the people of Canaan are still the same instructions we are to follow today. Lev. 18:3 **You must not do as they do in Egypt, where you used to live, and you must not do as they do in the land of Canaan, where I am bringing you. Do not follow their practices.** The culture of Canaan was cruel and horrific and God made it clear that there would be no mixing of these carnal practices while ministering to God.

True intimacy with God produces relational responsibility and a heartfelt desire to please the Lord. Similarly, when we express love to our spouses, we try to give them what makes their hearts glad and brings joy to their souls. Unlike becoming intimate with a wrong life partner whose attraction is mainly superficial, and all the inflamed emotions are hot and salacious in the first days of cohabitation, but later on, sadness and disappointment are the state of being because the love is not genuine of heart. Someone rightly said, "If you marry a child of the devil you are going to have problems with your father-in-law." You cannot serve two masters. We, the body of Christ, need to live in the culture of God's kingdom and set the standard for all cultures to gravitate and eventually become part of the Lord's loving gift of salvation. Our Heavenly Father must become the banner we live under. Jehovah Nissi - The Lord is my banner. Ex. 17:15 **Moses built an altar there and named it Yahweh-Nissi (which means "the LORD is my banner").** His banner over us is love, and the culture of God's kingdom has no cruelty within it.

At this time in our history, there is a vicious battle for the mind and the ownership of the culture's soul. Christianity would be an attractive choice if more Christians lived as Christians, and were not hell-bent on becoming spokesmen for the trends of society that draw Christians away from the foundational truth of the Gospel of Christ. If you have a passion for a particular segment of society that needs help, make sure that what that society stands for is not contrary to God's purposes and righteousness, or you will find yourself fighting against God, and that is a lose-lose situation.

Christ is the cornerstone of the culture that Christians abide by. We are the living stones in the Lord who are building the spiritual house of God through Christ. We cannot do this by bringing the corrupted culture of the world into God's holy building project. We have a mandate to keep cultural cruelty out of our testimony of love. 1Pet. 2:4 **As you come to Him, a living stone—rejected by people but chosen and honored by God—** 5 **You yourselves, as living stones, a spiritual house, are being built to be a holy priesthood to offer spiritual sacrifices acceptable to God through Jesus Christ.** This we will do when we seek God with all of our hearts.

Questions:

What have you allowed into your faith that you know God does not approve of?

_____

How can we meet the needs of the world but at the same time not become worldly?

_____

Frustrated Hope

Job 6:8 For oh that He would grant my desire, and my petition might come, and the Lord would grant my hope!

I thought aloud and said, "Why do I hope so much, and nothing comes of it?" I truly needed to ask myself whether I was living in the Lord's hope or simply wishing for things to happen. Hope gives life and power to faith, and if there is no faith coming forth as a result of our hope in God, it is all wishful thinking. We can find ourselves in the deepest oubliette of our making and become imprisoned by the hopelessness we are immersed in. Prov.13:12a **Delayed hope makes one sick at heart.** Delayed hope also creates an insouciant attitude toward hoping in the ability of God for one's life. Perhaps honest hope in God would allow us to see what God wants us to hope for in Him. Psalm 33:20 **We put our hope in the LORD. He is our help and our shield.**

The unintended consequence that can happen when we are frustrated in hope is that we start working out God's plan in our strength and creating a revision of our frustrated thoughts. Sarai was frustrated with God's plan and promise that she would have a child and become the mother of many nations. She eventually wrote her own action plan to help God along. Serai told Abram to have a child with Sarai's servant so that her frustration would go away (paraphrased). Gen. 16:2 **And Sarai said to Abram, "Behold now, the LORD has prevented me from bearing children. Go into my servant; it may be that I shall obtain children by her." And Abram listened to the voice of Sarai.** Of course, the legacy of Serai's frustrated hope resulted in a decision that is still felt today. Ishmael the offspring of Serai and Abram's selfish reasoning has been causing wars and strife throughout the Middle East and beyond to this day. Gen. 16:12 **This son of yours will be a wild** man, as untamed as a wild donkey! He will raise his fist against everyone, and everyone will be against him. Yes, he will live in open hostility against all his relatives.

King Saul had been instructed to utterly destroy the Amalekites and everything they owned,from the city and people, to the livestock. Because of fear and peer pressure, Saul rewrote the orders that the Lord had given him through the prophet Samuel. When Samuel eventually showed up he heard something that should not have been there. 1Sam. 15:14 **And Samuel said, "What then is this bleating of the sheep in my ears and the lowing of the oxen that I hear?"** Saul's frustration while waiting for Samuel created fear within his soul. Saul was afraid of the people, so he allowed the raiding party to bring the sheep and oxen as a sacrifice for the Lord. 1Sam. 15:24. **Saul said to Samuel, "I have sinned, for I have transgressed the commandment of the LORD and your words, because I feared the people and obeyed their voice.** The unintended consequence for Saul was that he would lose the kingdom to another who would follow God's instructions.

This is why we need to keep our hope in Christ and not in our capabilities to pull off the project. The Word of God is full of people who tried to do God's plan their way and only ended up with frustrated lives and hopelessness. Our confidence and hope need to be in the cross, and all that Christ did for us through His accepted sacrifice. We are never going to get it right by the constant observance of the law. This is why we needed a Saviour who satisfied the demands of the law through His blood. The law is a guide, instruction, or signpost that leads us to Christ, where we accept Him by faith. Gal. 3:24 **Let me put it another way. The law was our guardian until Christ came; it protected us until we could be made right with God through faith.** This is the fundamental difference between having my hope in God and wishing for stuff to happen.

Before I knew the Lord, I was separated from Him because of my sin and I had no eternal hope. I had an eternal existence, but no hope for that existence. Eph. 2:12 **That at that time you were separate from Christ, alienated from the commonwealth of Israel, and strangers to the covenants of the promise, not having hope and without God in the world.** Life was frustrating because the emptiness within my soul could not be filled by all I was wishing for. I needed a foundation that could only come through Christ the Lord. Once Jesus moved into my soul I could now hope in God and pray for the issues of life to be taken care of and I could do it by faith.

Do I still find myself in times of frustration? Yes, absolutely. However, I have a God-given plan for that frustration, and that is to settle down in the Lord's peace and begin to cast my cares upon Him. 1Pet. 5:7 **Cast all your anxiety on Him, because He cares for you.** After I cast my cares upon the Lord, then through prayer and faith in God's love for me, my frustration begins to wane, and the hope of glory revisits my heart and leads me to the promised land of God's goodness. If you are frustrated with life, spouse, friends, or existence then turn your eyes upon Jesus and hope in His grace that can heal all that ails your body, soul, and spirit. Psalm 43:5 **Why are you in despair, O my soul? And why are you disturbed within me? Hope in God, for I shall**

again praise Him, The help of my countenance and my God. Yes, hope in God!

Questions:

Have you ever gone ahead of God and tried to make the blessing or promise from God work now rather than wait for Him?

_____

What was the unintended consequence of your action?

_____

A Deal I Can Live With

Genesis 3:16 To the woman he said, "I will make your pains in childbearing very severe; with painful labour you will give birth to children. Your desire will be for your husband, and he will rule over you."

I was listening to a marriage counsellor describe some of the tools he uses when helping married couples try to reconcile their differences. He explained there would need to be compromises made by each spouse during the marriage to make the union work. Some of the questions from the audience were interesting because of the diversity of issues. Where one couple had no problems in a particular wife-husband role, another couple could not come to terms with the same scenario. They could not arrive at a deal they could live with. Money, emotional support, and children were the main subjects of contention that were leading some to file for divorce. Compromising to help save a marriage at the point of contention had become difficult because the personal slights, imagined or real, had become a battleground to be fought over. Prov. 18:19 **An offended friend is harder to win back than a fortified city. Arguments separate friends like a gate locked with bars.**

There were many other problems, like infidelity, dysfunctional in laws, and life-changing addictions that were reasons for calling it quits, but suffice it to say the human stamina and grit it takes to find a resolution a couple can live with has become a challenge in this difficult and contentious world. Unless we appropriate the promises of God by faith and use our faith to heal our marriages, there will always be destructive behaviours within unions and the need for marriage counsellors. What so many Christians have forgotten is that the curse that was proclaimed in the Garden of Eden is still part of the problem couples have been fighting with their whole lives. The question is, what made this part of the curse such a problem? Gen. 3:16b **Your desire will be for your husband, and he will rule over you."**

When God said, "Your desire will be for your husband," this statement resulted in a terrible place for Eve to find herself. Whatever God had fulfilled in her heart and soul by His love and presence before sin, was now going to be looked for and expected to be filled in her husband. The assurance and affirmation that came from God through true love, would now be sought after in her spouse. How could Adam or any husband fulfill what God had perfectly provided for in the deepest part of a human's soul? Plus there was the added part of the curse that Adam would be under. Cursed was the ground or system that would provide for them. Gen. 3:17 **And to the man he said, "Since you listened to your wife and ate from the tree whose fruit I commanded you not to eat, the ground is cursed because of you. All your life you will struggle to scratch a living from it. 18 It will produce thorns and thistles for you, and you will eat the plants of the field.**

So now, this poor sap of a husband has to work under the curse of a hard life—from having a terrible job, poor management, and being underpaid to CEOs raiding his pension funds and working in a world-rigged financial system. And on top of it, he is carrying the burden of his wife's physical, emotional, and maternal needs that only God can fulfill. Talk about the weight of the whole world on his shoulders. How cursed is that? Some translations say that *she will desire to control her husband, but he will rule over her.* All these desires to dominate the situation are all part of the curse. A wife's desire to control her husband is not all her fault. In most cases, she is only trying to find the lost fulfilling friendship she had with her creator's ability to meet those deep needs, and it falls short when her husband comes across as someone who can barely get to work on time to meet up with his own curse.

I've been asked by a few women, "Why is my mother trying to control my husband? This is causing trouble in the family." Again, this is one of the tentacles from the same curse at work. Whether a mother-in-law is widowed or divorced the same seeking of soul-peace is now being looked for in her daughter's husband. What a cycle of unattainable fulfilment. The only way to have that monumental emptiness fulfilled is to find the way back to the relationship that was normal and natural in the Garden of Eden before sin had corrupted everything wherever man existed. This cursed earth that humanity is trying to find peace in is groaning over the sins of mankind. Rom. 8:22 **For we know that all creation has been groaning as in the pains of childbirth right up to the present time.**

Is there hope? Yes, yes, yes there is! Thank God the scriptures point out that this warfare is not with our spouses or inlaws but we are wrestling demonic forces, and it is those forces that are provoking all the angst and scrambled inner feelings. Eph. 6:12 **For we are not fighting against flesh-and-blood enemies, but against evil rulers and authorities of the unseen world, against mighty powers in this dark world, and against evil spirits in the heavenly places.** One of the gifts of salvation in Christ that we have been given is restoration in fellowship with our heavenly Father through Jesus Christ the Son of God. What we men need to do, is to use our faith in Christ, and with prayer, find our fulfilment in the one who created us and knows exactly how to heal the inner man of our being.

As men in Christ, we can now declare gratefulness, offer prayers for company management, and allow God to protect our future and make whatever we do prosper unto the Lord. In Christ, we can ask for insight into creating companies and inventions that are needed on this earth. Through our faith, we can become satisfied and thankful for what we have and can sit with God asking for His leadership in this precarious world. By faith in Christ, the men can move out of the curse's reach and become husbands and fathers who rule justly in home life, work life and citizenry. The women who accept the Lord's fulfilling love and the presence of their Saviour in their hearts can now be at peace in their souls because their faith is at work submitting to God's loving and fulfilling will. Now, the married couple can be helpmates to each other and not competitors of power. Eph. 5:31 **For this reason a man will leave his father and mother and be united to his wife, and the two will become one flesh.**

As the expression states, a family who prays together stays together. A husband who thanks God for his wife, will have God sowing the deep-hearted love his wife needs to be and feel complete as a woman. A wife who comes to God interceding for her husband will be given the words of wisdom that will confirm the family is whole and wholly righteous through Christ unto God. Will there be trials and tribulations during the married couple's life? There will be hardships to work out. However, if God is the center of their marriage and honest hearts are submitted to God and each other, then the world will have a hard time trying to break them up. Now that is a deal I can live with.

Question:

What compromises did you make that helped a situation in your relationship?

_____

_____

Do It Afraid

Joshua 1:9 Have I not commanded you? Be strong and courageous. Do not be frightened, and do not be dismayed, for the Lord your God is with you wherever you go."

I was working out on the rings at the gym, and someone came up to me and pointed out the dangers of getting hurt (for someone my age). The implication is that I should be more afraid of hurting myself because I'm older than most of the people at the gym and it can take longer to heal if I get hurt. I thought, sometimes new routines can be challenging and there are moments of uncertainty, but I just do it afraid until I'm not. Then eventually, I've got the new routine down. I think that goes for anything in life. How do we overcome fear and life's obstacles unless we are experiencing them and learning how to defeat them? The explorers and trailblazers would never have gone anywhere had they not gone out to the wild unknown. Had they allowed fear to stop them from overcoming all the odds against them, they would not have accomplished anything. We all need to have a trailblazing attitude toward the things that scare us, otherwise, we will never go forward and overcome anything worth accomplishing.

The word *overcome* implies that there will be a struggle to conquer something challenging or sometimes fearful. We need to overcome the fears and challenges of life. We were created to face confrontations, hardships, and difficulties by finding ways to keep our lives and bodies healthy, wise, and inquisitive through the hardships of life. We were created to create. With God's directions, we were created to take charge of the world and manage it for the good of all. Gen. 1:26 **Then God said, "Let Us make man in Our image, according to Our likeness; and let them rule over the fish of the sea and over the birds of the sky and over the cattle and over all the earth, and over every creeping thing that creeps on the earth."**

Whether we realize it or not, there is a lot of responsibility in ruling over all of creation. Some of the world's events and scenarios are going to cause fear and present an opportunity to be afraid just because of the overwhelming difficulty of managing it all. We will need to learn to do it afraid until we are not. Knowing that the Lord is encouraging us forward will help us rule by faith. Will we make mistakes? We sure will, but with God, we will improve in our decision-making. Isa. 41:13 **For I, the Lord your God, hold your right hand; it is I who say to you, "Fear not, I am the one who helps you."**

The Lord asks us to spread the good news of not needing to live in a constant state of fear. Isa. 35:4 **Say to those who have an anxious heart, "Be strong; fear not! Behold, your God will come with vengeance, with the recompense of God. He will come and save you."** Yes, we can be strong in the Lord. When the children of Israel were stuck between the Red Sea and Pharaoh's chariots coming fast upon them, fear was the prevalent feeling among the people. Ex. 14:10 **When Pharaoh drew near, the people of Israel lifted up their eyes, and behold, the Egyptians were marching after them, and they feared greatly. And the people of Israel cried out to the LORD.** They were afraid but had to overcome the fear by believing

God's word of deliverance given to them through Moses. Ex. 14:13 **Moses answered the people, "Do not be afraid. Stand firm and you will see the deliverance the LORD will bring you today. The Egyptians you see today you will never see again**. They might have been apprehensive to go forward but they went through the Red Sea on dry land and did it afraid until they were not.

The Psalmist says it best. Psalm 27:1 **The Lord is my light and my salvation— whom shall I fear? The Lord is the stronghold of my life—of whom shall I be afraid?** What have you partnered with that keeps you in fear? We are encouraged to let the Lord be the stronghold of our souls so that we overcome fear. If you have partnered with anything other than God to get through life, then chances are you will struggle and be fearful most of the time. The Lord has not given us a spirit of fear. Christ Jesus has given us His redemptive strength to be courageous in the battle of life. Plus, He has given us His armour to wear so that we defeat the attacks of the enemy that will come our way. Eph. 6:10 **Finally, be strong in the Lord and in the strength of his might. 11 Put on the full armour of God, so that you can take your stand against the devil's schemes**.

It is God's will that we learn to trust Him when He says not to fear and believe that He is going to be with us wherever we go. Josh. 1:9 **Have I not commanded you? Be strong and courageous. Do not be frightened, and do not be dismayed, for the Lord your God is with you wherever you go."** For a lot of people, this is going to be a hard thing to learn and believe. Therefore, do it afraid until you are not. Learn to grow in faith and become trusting in your relationship with the Lord until one day you are declaring, "I will not be afraid!" Psalm 118:6 **The Lord is with me; I will not be afraid. What can mere mortals do to me?**

Question:

What was one of the most difficult things God asked you to do and you did it while being afraid?

_____

_____

Norm-Isms

You are called to be the best version of who you are in Christ.

We are all hypocritical but too hypocritical to admit it.

Make yourself accountable.

Part Three
Faithful In Heart

There is a lot of talk about being faithful, and many books have been written on how to try to be faithful, or at least give it an honest attempt. Faithfulness comes from that place within the soul that wants to express gratitude for being alive. It is not so much a step one, then step two approach to being faithful and accountable that makes it work. It takes a willing heart and discipline to be faithful. Therefore, we had better know the One we are being faithful to and for what reason we have put out hope. Jesus is Lord and was faithful in giving His life for my soul. I can be faithful to Him because He gave me everything.

Group Therapy

James 5:16 Confess your faults one to another, and pray one for another, that ye may be healed. The effectual fervent prayer of a righteous man availeth much.

I listened to a psychologist explaining the difference between one-on-one therapy versus group therapy. He explained that group therapy brought about better healing results, and a greater percentage of people becoming healed of the multiple mental illnesses and issues they were suffering from. He said that one-on-one therapy was harder to obtain good results because the people were much more prone to being self-centred during the therapy session than those in the group sessions. The therapist explained that in a group environment, there was empathy among those within the group toward the others needing help. They discovered there was genuine help for the mentally ill in the group because some of the people in that grouping had gone through the same problems. Plus there was a feeling of acceptance once people began to share the mental issues that needed healing within their lives.

I found the interview with the psychologist interesting because, in effect, the psychologist confirmed that the church was doing the same thing and had been doing it every week for centuries. The words explaining the group settings differed, but the results were similar. What we as Christians call fellowship, is in effect a form of spiritual group therapy. The Word of God admonishes us to remain faithful in coming together regularly and to keep our hearts ready to repent and change our minds when we receive anointed guidance from the Holy Spirit. The result is that we can walk in the healing Word of God and be a blessing to those struggling in life. Heb. 10:25 **And let us not neglect our meeting together, as some people do, but encourage one another, especially now that the day of his return is drawing near.**

It has been said that many are communicating but not many are connecting. Could it be that everyone is talking and no one is listening? I believe there is a worldwide need for people to connect on an emotional level because the loneliness that is prevalent among the youth and elderly has become a universal problem. Maybe it was not such a good idea to create a system where the elderly were housed in care homes, the young were planted in daycare, and never the two would meet. The Word of the Lord says to let the children come to Him and that the elderly would bear fruit in old age. Might God have been thinking that the elderly having a strong relationship with Him, could have ministered with patient love to the young who have thousands of questions that only the elderly would patiently answer, and might have fixed the loneliness problem?

We do need to come together in Godly support groups. The first church was a collection of home groups and a place where the new believers in Christ would meet and pray. Rom. 16:5a **Likewise greet the church that is in their house.** There is power when we pray together. When two or more are gathered together with Christ as the group's center, we can bring our petitions to God the Father. Matt. 18:20 **For where two or three are gathered together in My name, I am there in the midst of them.** There is strength in numbers when brothers and sisters in the Lord are believing God together for a united purpose that is God's will. The power of a group of righteous men and women who believe God can become a formidable force and can create a unity that is hard to break. Eccl. 4:12b **A cord of three strands is not quickly torn apart.**

The Lord has put within salvation the gift of healing for all people who accept God's gift of forgiveness. The Lord encourages us to submit to one another in the faith and to be a blessing to each other. We become strengthened and encouraged in Christ by confessing our faults to one another and praying for one another. This congregational type of group involvement helps us take care of each other and also reminds us that we all require God's help at all times. James 5:16 **Confess your**

faults one to another, and pray one for another, that ye may be healed. The effectual fervent prayer of a righteous man availeth much.

For those who think that they can make it through this world without the nurturing of other fellow believers might want to look to the wild animal kingdom to see what happens when a predator separates a weakling or even a lone water buffalo from the group. Yes, the water buffalo is big and strong, but not strong enough when a pack of predators sets their mind to take it down. We have an evil enemy who goes around as a roaring lion seeking whom he may devour. Satan looks for the ones who have become separated from fellowship and group prayer. Stay in touch with the believers in Christ and the elders in the church, as well as the congregants who can help keep each other accountable to the Lord Jesus. Don't be afraid to ask for prayer when going through difficult times, and be ready to pray and be a blessing when others ask you to cover their lives in anointed intercession. Keep showing up to God's group therapy and grow mentally strong as well as spiritually strong in Him who first loved us.

Questions:

Do you find it hard to connect with people?

_____

If not, what is your strategy for making the encounter with people count?

_____

Becoming Cancelable

Malachi 3:13 Your words have been hard against me, says the Lord. But you say, 'How have we spoken against you?' 14 You have said, 'It is vain to serve God. What is the profit of our keeping his charge or of walking as in mourning before the Lord of hosts?

When we become the target of harsh and negative words, it can feel like we have had a big rubber stamp punched across our forehead that says, *"Canceled."* Many ministers go through this hardship and feel like they have become cancelable. Once called upon to help in an emergency, now chucked to the broom closet because the emergency is over. Once a needed pastor who gave sage advice and direction is now considered a *pester* and not a *pastor,* who should mind their own business.

Ministers in positions of leading assemblies, counselling the heartbroken and ill, while directing those needing help in life, often receive desperate phone calls or frantic whispered encounters in the church lobby from people who have messed up their lives and are now begging for help to escape the consequences of their sinful choices. "I'll do whatever it takes to get my life in order," are the promises made in those moments of desperation. The amount of prayer, dedication, late nights studying, and spiritual strength it takes for honest ministers to fortify their hearts to become the helpers the fallen need, is unexplainable to those who think ministers and what they do are no big deal. The facts are, that the minister's soul is invested in those they are helping and it can be a brutal awakening when these same pastors are shoved to the side because the fallen no longer want to go forward after all the promises of solicitude were made in desperation. Mal. 3:14 **You have said, 'It is vain to serve God. What is the profit of our keeping his charge or of walking as in mourning before the Lord of hosts?**

Even God can become cancelable in people's lives. God had led the children of Israel to the Promised Land and years after the Israelites had lived in the land, their ungratefulness toward God became evident when they declared they wanted to be ruled by a king rather than a judge whom God had appointed over them. Samuel took it personally that he was being cancelled, but God pointed out to Samuel that the people were rejecting God Himself, and not Samuel's leadership. 1Sam. 8:7 **And the LORD said to Samuel, "Listen to the voice of the people in all that they say to you. For it is not you they have rejected, but they have rejected Me as their king.**

Someone might say, "How can you cancel God from your life when He has done so much for you?" We do not need to look far than to our own lives to see that we have done it on many occasions. Every time we willfully sin, we do it. Every time we reject the Word of the Lord that comes our way when we are in trouble, we do it. I have experienced this when I have been asked for help in different situations and when victory is just over the turbulent horizon, some of those being helped just cancel me out and say, "Thanks, I got this, you can leave me alone now," and like that—*Cancelled.* I'm not looking for praise or validation that I, and I alone, got these souls through their mess because we all know it was God leading us through the circumstances together that brought the opportunity for victory—if the people continue in the Word. However, it can hit our soul very hard if we are not wearing the armour of God that protects us from all fiery darts regardless of where the darts came from.

What I am pointing out, is that being cancelled is going to be part of life for those who serve in any capacity of ministry. Whether a pastor, minister, civil servant, politician, or medical practitioner—you will be rejected and cancelled by the very people you are helping. This is why we need to love the Lord more than the accolades of people because it is the love and joy of the Lord that will keep us in the strength and courage we need to finish what God has called us to do. The gratitude and the thank yous that come our way are nice and many times uplifting, but our real strength comes from God and Him only. The accolades of the crowd can lead people to start believing in their own press, and major missteps begin to happen when man's ego becomes their god. Luke 6:26 **Woe to you when all men speak well of you, for their fathers treated the false prophets in the same way.**

Jesus had a similar event happen to Him as what happened to His Heavenly Father. Isa. 53:3a **He was despised and rejected by men, a man of sorrows, acquainted with grief.** God had been rejected and cancelled from a nation's consciousness as He pointed out to Samuel. Similarly, one day Jesus is being hailed with shouts of, "Hosanna in the highest," and not long after, the same people are screaming, "Crucify Him to death!" Luke 23:21 **But they shouted, saying, "Crucify Him, crucify Him!"** This is fickle behaviour for a people who claim to be following God.

Our stability in the faith comes from our ability to obey and stick with what the Holy Spirit is showing us through His Word. Our strength grows from the Lord's approval and love that He lavishes upon us. Our lives become filled with grace, when we keep coming to God the Father for His mercy to be given to us and lived through, as we face all the hate the world freely gives out to all. Truly God is good. Let us not worry about being cancelled, but rather, let us trust God with all our hearts and He will give us His assurance and rest.

Question:

How did you feel when someone you mentored eventually matured and went on in life?

Serving In The Shadow of Others

Romans 16:3 Greet Priscilla and Aquila my helpers in Christ Jesus: 4 Who risked their own necks for my life, to whom not only I give thanks, but also all the churches of the Gentiles.

The list of people that the Apostle Paul gives recognition in Romans Chapter sixteen are people who accepted the Lord Jesus as Saviour and lived out their lives the best they could. These people served and helped establish the Kingdom of God. We need to know that serving in the shadows of others does not go unnoticed in the eyes of God. Many times we place importance on certain ministry functions that are up there or out there in front where everyone can see. The big stage and those who minister from it are often revered as more special than others. This is so far from the truth and yet people keep falling for the lies of the enemy who consistently points out that what you are doing isn't much in the Kingdom of God compared to others. Therein is the first problem—comparing ourselves to others. 2Cor. 10:12 **We do not dare to classify or compare ourselves with some who commend themselves. When they measure themselves by themselves and compare themselves with themselves, they show their ignorance.**

A man, who is recorded as Abraham's servant, covenanted with Abraham to seek out a wife for Isaac whom Abraham and God would approve. Through humble prayer, this servant was led to Rebekah who accepted the arranged offer of marriage with Isaac. This servant served in Abraham's house, but God used him to make sure the Abrahamic covenant continued. Talk about serving in the shadow of a patriarch and yet the servant's role in history is profound. Gen. 24:2 **Abraham said to his servant, the elder of his household who managed all he owned, "Place your hand under my thigh,** 3 **"and I will have you swear by the LORD, God of heaven and God of earth, that you will not take a wife for my son from the daughters of the Canaanites among whom I live,** 4 **"but will go to my land and my family to take a wife for my son Isaac."**

Samuel was a young boy who served Eli the Prophet of God. Samuel was serving everyone who worked in the temple. Eli's sons were corrupt and treated the office of ministry with contempt. 1Sam. 2:17 **Thus the sin of the young men was very great in the sight of the LORD, for the men treated the offering of the LORD with contempt.** They might have held the title of priests, but God used Samuel to bring the word of judgment that exposed all the crimes being committed in the temple. 1Sam. 3:13 **And I declare to him that I am about to punish his house forever, for the iniquity that he knew, because his sons were blaspheming God, and he did not restrain them.** Samuel served in the shadow of a prophet and priests who were at best showing up for temple duty and at worst corrupting the representation of God, and yet, Samuel grew in the blessings and favour of the Lord.

Simon of Cyrene was minding his own business coming into town from the country when he was forced to carry the Lord's cross. Luke 23:26 **And when they led Him away, they seized a man, Simon of Cyrene, as he was coming in from the country, and placed on him the cross to carry behind Jesus.** I am speculating here, as I think about the cruel procession Simon came across when he saw the man, Jesus, struggling under the weight of His cross. Suddenly, a Roman soldier forced Simon to pick up the Lord's cross and become part of the horrific procession. To the spectators, Simon looked like he was participating in the crucifixion of Jesus, but in reality, by carrying the cross for the Lord, this action was the only grace Jesus experienced for a few moments by having the weight of the world taken off His shoulders. Simon found himself serving by carrying the cross which would also be the way for Simon to receive salvation and deliverance from his sins.

Simon of Cyrene carried the very cross that the

curse of mankind's sins would be nailed to. Do not ever discount the small or sometimes inconvenient things God asks you to do. Rom. 16:6 **Greet Mary, who worked very hard for you.** All of us who are walking with the Lord, are the result of someone tirelessly doing the things God asked them to do. Whether it was volunteering for kids camp for one summer, or warmly greeting someone at a church assembly entrance, these services are accumulating to a greater work that only God can see the total result. Rom. 16:9 **Greet Urbanus, our coworker in Christ, and my dear friend Stachys.**

As the Prophet Zechariah points out, not to despise small beginnings or the things that seem to be small advancements, or little stuff in comparison to the big picture. Zeck. 4:10a **Do not despise these small beginnings, for the LORD rejoices to see the work begin.** Don't let the enemy of your soul make you feel less than the king and priest you are in Christ. The devil is so jealous of the position you own in the love of God. Satan boils with hate when God looks at what you do for Him and acknowledges your faithfulness with blessings upon your life. Rom. 16:12 **Salute Tryphena and Tryphosa, who labour in the Lord. Salute the beloved Persis, which laboured much in the Lord.** All these ordinary people whom Paul is acknowledging were people like you and me who decided to serve in the shadows of others. Let us keep doing the work that God asks us to do and give Him praise as we do it. Blessings be upon us all.

Questions:

Has your service to God and His kingdom been rewarding to you?

_____

Have you found it difficult to submit when God asks you to do hard tasks?

_____

Things On My Heart

Proverbs 4:23 Above all else, guard your heart, for everything you do flows from it.

The things God has planted in your heart are important, and if you sense a burden to fulfill them, then you need to pick up the challenge. I was talking with my publisher Clay, and he is concerned that he is working too much in the areas that are not as important as what God had sown in his heart to do and accomplish within the Lord's Kingdom. That is something we all need to be concerned about. As my friend Jami Rogers explains it, "We have been given an allotted amount of time on this earth to fulfill the story God is telling about Himself through us." Christ who lives within our hearts, is shepherding us toward what God the Father created us to be, and fulfill. We can only do this with Jesus at the helm of our hearts. Acts 17:28a **For in Him we live, and move, and have our being**.

A lot of Christians are struggling with what they perceive as not having a vision from or for God. They seem to believe there has to be a burning-bush experience or a thunderclap attention-getter, thinking this is how God communicates His desires. The Holy Spirit speaks through a still small voice and in heartfelt impressions. Sometimes God will simply give you an impression of wanting to be a blessing in a certain situation, but because we mistakenly think that we will be inconvenienced or the person will reject our offer, we put off what was just on our heart as a fleeting feeling, and we start wondering if we did hear from God.

I was walking out of a hardware store and a heavy rain began to fall. There is a bus stop right near the parking lot I was parked in, and there was a blind man who I recognized standing and getting wet while waiting for a bus. The thing on my heart was that I should offer him a ride and as I was thinking this thought, the clear soft voice of the Lord said, "Offer him a ride to where he is going." Here is the rub. I felt I should do it and there was a strong conviction to offer the ride but I was supposed to be at a bank appointment in fifteen minutes. My heart was saying to offer help but my mind was wrestling because of a possible inconvenience to me time-wise.

The quiet voice of God prevailed and I asked the man if he needed a ride. He thanked me for the offer and told me where he was going. I said, "Hey I'm headed in that direction." I smiled and repented to God for having thoughts about this man being an inconvenience. The fact was that the blind man was going to the bank across the street from the one I was going to. Yeah, I felt a bit foolish because the thing in my heart was to give this man some help but I started getting distracted from what God had sown within me because I started second-guessing God's request by allowing selfishness to make the bank appointment more important. No lightning flashes or trumpet sounds from heaven declaring to the world God had asked me to do something for Him. Just a still small voice putting a desire in my heart to help. 1Kings 19:12 **After the earthquake came a fire, but the LORD was not in the fire. And after the fire came a gentle whisper. 13a So it was, when Elijah heard it.**

We can see the immediate effect that Jesus' words had on the disciple's hearts. Jesus walked by them and after speaking these simple words, "Follow me," caused the disciples to respond right at that moment. There are things of God and desires that show up in our hearts that cause us to search out the depth of what the Holy Spirit is sowing within us. It is as if Jesus had just walked by and said, "These are the things you are going to want to do and will find fulfilling pleasure in them, therefore, guard your heart so that you can hear My voice clearly." Prov. 4:23 **Above all else, guard your heart, for everything you do flows from it.**

How did Jesus find out what was on His Heavenly Father's heart? What allowed Jesus to keep saying that He and the Father were one and on the same page? Through prayer, Jesus chose the apostles out of the disciples who were following Him. Luke 6:12 **During those days he went out to the mountain to pray and spent all night in prayer to God. 13 When daylight came, he summoned his disciples, and he chose twelve of them, whom he also named apostles.** There came a day when the disciples would have to do what was on their hearts and commit fully to the calling that had been placed within them. It is the same for us. We start walking with the Lord because we responded to God's love and we became born again. Then, as we mature in Christ, through obedient prayer to our Heavenly Father, we begin to understand and keep the things God has placed in our hearts. May we all respond with peace to what God is leading our hearts to do, and who we are to be in Him.

Question:

What has God put on your heart that you are waiting for Him to fulfil?

What Are You Buying Into?

Revelation 3:18 I counsel you to buy from Me gold having been refined by fire so that you may be rich, and white garments so that you may be clothed and the shame of your nakedness might not be made manifest, and eye-salve to anoint your eyes so that you may see.

I have noticed the targeted advertising since my seventieth birthday. The multiple ads on my social media and email platforms have been inviting me to consider free consultations for hearing aids, mobility vehicles, automatic prescription refills, retirement homes, very expensive life insurance, and yes, funeral arrangements. Gone are the ads for fast cars, family vacations, easy financing, and timeshares. Just like that, after a birthday date and at the flip of a switch, I'm being sold the joys of death and dying. The question is, do I buy into it? I have had to consider two questions lately: What are they selling, and what am I buying into? These are the two questions I need to give serious thought to, as the foundations of the world tremble and shake. Change on a cataclysmic scale is rushing at all of us, and we need to know what we are being driven toward.

What I need to do is keep buying into what God is giving me, especially now that I am three score and ten. As I get older I love the idea that God can still use me for His kingdom work. Psalm 92:12 **The righteous will flourish like a palm tree, they will grow like a cedar of Lebanon; 13 planted in the house of the LORD, they will flourish in the courts of our God. 14 They will still bear fruit in old age, they will stay fresh and green, 15 proclaiming, "The LORD is upright; he is my Rock, and there is no wickedness in him."** There it is, Saints. I will bear fruit in old age as I proclaim that the Lord is my rock and He is my righteousness. I don't even need to be concerned about my gray hair. I can thank God for it and be at peace, as I walk in the glory of His righteousness. Prov. 16:31 **Gray hair is a crown of glory; it is gained by living a godly life.**

The question remains—am I going to buy into what the world is selling me or am I going to buy into what God has given me through His eternal gift and sacrifice that came through Christ's crucifixion? Eternal value versus temporary existence—that is the question. How do we balance our lives while living on this precarious earth, and aim our heart's love toward eternity with our God? It comes down to what we are going to put our confidence in. What are we bowing our hearts toward and where are we storing our heavenly treasures? Matt. 6:19 **Do not store up for yourselves treasures on earth, where moths and vermin destroy, and where thieves break in and steal.** 20 **But store up for yourselves treasures in heaven, where moths and vermin do not destroy, and where thieves do not break in and steal.**

The Lord instructs us to buy from Him gold having been refined by His fire. The Lord is asking us to allow His Spirit to burn the dross out of our hearts so that we may wear His robe of righteousness without shame. God wants us to walk as the kings and priests we are, and stop buying into the counterfeit self-righteousness the enemy of our soul is selling us. Rev. 3:18 **I counsel you to buy from Me gold having been refined by fire so that you may be rich, and white garments so that you may be clothed and the shame of your nakedness might not be made manifest, and eye-salve to anoint your eyes so that you may see.**

Eve bought a bill of goods that Satan was selling. Eve was the original woman who had everything. She had a husband and companion, a garden that supplied all her needs, and the security of a relationship with God the creator of the universe. Yet Satan was able to sell her a concept that she was missing something in her life that God was keeping from her. Gen. 3:5 **For God knows that when you eat from it your eyes will be opened, and you will be like God, knowing good and evil.** Eve was already created in God's image but bought the lie that she was less than who God made her to be. Satan is still selling this lie today.

The nation of Israel bought into the idea that having a king to rule over them was better than having a man of God rule through God's instructions. They were influenced by what they saw around them and started comparing themselves to their neighbouring kingdoms. Comparing ourselves to others is never a good idea because we lose the identity God gave us. 1Sam. 8:5 **They said to him, "Look, you are old, and your sons do not walk in your ways. Therefore, appoint a king to judge us the same as all the other nations have."** As a nation, they bought into a political idea that resulted in rejecting God as their leader and sovereign King. 1Sam. 8:7 **And the LORD said to Samuel, "Obey the voice of the people in all that they say to you, for they have not rejected you, but they have rejected me from being king over them**. Israel suffered greatly for this choice and had to live with the consequences of rejecting God.

Judas Iscariot was paid in silver to buy into the plan of betraying Jesus. This apostle had so much opportunity because he walked with the divine Saviour of the world. Yet somehow betraying his Lord became a good idea. Did the sin Judas agree to take part in become an easy choice because he had already crossed a moral line by stealing from the money bag? John 12:6 **Judas did not say this because he cared about the poor, but because he was a thief. As keeper of the money bag, he used to take from what was put into it**. The consequence of unrepented sin normally leads to more sin.

We all need to pay attention to what we are buying into. The world is full of alternative ideas and views on what and who they think God is and who He should be. We are being sold an agenda that results in humanism and self-righteousness. Keep buying the gold refined by the Lord, and focus on walking with Him. Keep an eye on what you are being sold. If what is being sold does not set you free in Christ, then ditch it.

Questions:

What product have you bought that has given you buyer's remorse?

_____

What did God try to get you to put your heart into that you delayed doing and now regret?

_____

Smile And Nod

Romans 12:18 If it is possible, as much as depends on you, live peaceably with all men.

I was talking with my mom about some family dynamics that were not going to be easy to deal with. I asked her how she dealt with these types of situations, and she said, "I have learned to just smile and nod, nod and smile." I started laughing and said, "That would make things simple." Just don't pick it up and place the problem in your heart or don't let it live rent-free in your mind—just smile and nod and let it go. There comes a point in many family situations where you will not be able to fix everything that comes your way. I've said this before, "I think God gives us good friends to make up for the family members He gave us." For some family members, it will not matter what you say. The fact that you said something will only stir up greater anger, anxiety, and belligerence. To smile and nod may be the only thing you can do while you silently pray for them. Only God can fix dysfunction.

King David was dealing with family problems in his life. We read in, 2Samuel 16, where Shimei came out cursing at King David and spouting nonsense. 2Sam. **16:5 As King David approached Bahurim, a man from the family of the house of Saul was just coming out. His name was Shimei son of Gera, and as he approached, he kept yelling out curses. 6 He threw stones at David and all the servants of the king, though the troops and all the mighty men were on David's right and left. 7 And as he yelled curses, Shimei said, "Get out, get out, you worthless man of bloodshed! 8 The LORD has paid you back for all the blood of the house of Saul, in whose place you have reigned, and the LORD has delivered the kingdom into the hand of your son Absalom. See, you have come to ruin because you are a man of bloodshed!"**

Like many of us who need to face, referee, or tolerate family issues that can become big family dramas and misunderstandings, King David was dealing with difficult family dynamics. Absalom, David's son, was strategizing a coup against David's reign over Israel. After listening to all the cursing that was coming out of Shimei, one of David's men suggested they silence the accuser by cutting off his head. 2Sam. 16:9 **Then Abishai son of Zeruiah said to the king, "Why should this dead** dog curse my lord the king? Let me go over and cut off his head!"** However, David decides to let God deal with it and says, 2Sam. 16:12 **Perhaps the LORD will see my affliction and repay me with good for the cursing I receive today."** Another way of looking at it, David just smiled and nodded while allowing God the space to bring about His will for that situation.

Not only in families, but I believe this is why we have misunderstandings in the church as well. The Word of the Lord describes us as brothers and sisters in Christ, and thus by default, we become part of the church family. Not all brothers and sisters get along and differences of opinion will cause friction. Therefore, Paul the Apostle rightly says to get along as best as you can. Rom. 12:18 **If it is possible, as much as depends on you, live peaceably with all men.** As the Word says, "As long as it depends on you, live peacefully." Like everyone else, I must be ready to smile and nod so that we may get along as much as possible and be someone dependable not to start a brawl in the church lobby. Hopefully, the antics and fighting that have become commonplace in big box store parking lots do not become a scene in church parking lots.

When Jesus walked the earth, His earthly family misunderstood Him. His brothers thought he was self-centred when in fact, Jesus was Heavenly Father-centred. The Lord's brothers misunderstood Him and thought He was trying to gain worldly status—to get as many likes as possible on His religious channel so to speak. John 7:3 **Jesus' brothers said to him, "Leave Galilee and go to Judea, so that your disciples there may see the works you do. 4 No one who wants to become a public figure acts in secret. Since you are doing these**

things, show yourself to the world." 5 For even his brothers did not believe in him. Jesus was doing His Heavenly Father's will, and it was causing friction within the family. Jesus had to smile and nod while saying to his brothers, John 7:8 **Go up to the feast on your own. I am not going up to this feast, because My time has not yet come**.

You can imagine the talk the Lord's brothers were having as they went to the religious feast. They must have sounded like so many of us when complaining about the problems in our families. "Who does Super Brother think He is? Why is it always about Him? For once, can't He think of someone else besides Himself and His God of Israel? It's always Abba Abba Abba with Him. Mom never says anything, she just ponders the things He says in her heart, but if we or our sisters say anything against Him, she is all over us." Does this sound familiar? Maybe there are some offences we need to repent about. Prov. 18:19 **A brother offended is harder to be won than a strong city, And contentions are like the bars of a citadel.**

There is a time to speak and say something when the situation becomes dangerous or detrimental to other family members, but so often being right can be overrated when it is for all the small stuff that just doesn't matter. Maybe a bit more smiling and nodding would calm a lot of things down. Yes, you can claim to know your family because you grew up with them, but only God knows the heart of each person in your family. Let God deal with them as we keep them in our prayers and hopefully, the family is keeping you in their prayers. After all, you may be the reason they are all smiling and nodding just to keep the peace. We are all trying to get through this life with the least amount of grief possible. Everyone needs grace. It took my mom over eighty years to perfect the idea of smiling and nodding. Maybe we can learn it sooner. God bless us all.

Question:

Do you find it difficult to let things go when they are said, or can you just smile and nod and let it go?

Based On A True Story

1John 5:20 And we know that the Son of God has come and has given us understanding, so that we may know Him who is true; and we are in Him who is true—in His Son Jesus Christ. He is the true God and eternal life.

Whenever there is a movie that is advertised as *Based on a true story*, chances are the result will be nothing like the true story that truly happened. The production studios will have whitewashed the story to suit their loose interpretation, budgets, and the audience's ability to follow the narrative. We have all read a book about the true events that captured our hearts, causing great thoughts of inspiration, enlightening our ability to understand, and bringing us to places we never thought possible. Then one day, we hear a movie is coming out based on our favourite authentic story and we already know in our hearts that it will be a hack job by the time it is available for viewing.

This type of rewriting of history is taking place right under our noses. We need to do the fact-checking of dates and who said certain things, but not rewrite and eliminate whole parts of the nasty, evil, and corrupt events we as a nation took part in. We can be proud of our country as we improve as a society, but we need to face the wrongs that were done so that we do not repeat the brutality of what was once considered acceptable behaviour. We get rid of our sins when we confess them and repent of them. It is no different for nations. Nations must also repent of their sinful wrongs.

What we are witnessing is not a conspiracy theory. We are watching the narrative of certain historical events being rewritten to suit the ideology of certain factions of society. We are seeing a strategic plan to deny true historical events like the Holocaust, where six million Jewish souls were murdered. Recently some of the anti-Semitic hate speech has been expressed in this manner, "It was only about a hundred thousand killed and not six million." Oh, I see, that makes it all nice and forthright because there were ONLY a hundred thousand people murdered in the name of nationalism. Yeah right, just rewrite the historical evils that were done to suit the capacity of our callous heart's tolerance to accept a level of evil one can live with. Talk about ignorance gone to seed. Matt. 24:12 **And because lawlessness is to be multiplied, the love of the many will grow cold.**

To deny that slavery, residential school child abuse, war crimes, and genocide toward large people groups truly happened, will only place us in a position to repeat these same atrocities all over again. If on a national scale, these sins are not acknowledged and repented of with an honest heart, then history will repeat. Just because the horrible events of our nation's past do not sit well with those who do not want to face the true story of the maliciousness their ancestors took part in, is not a case for denying these iniquities took place. It happened, so what are we going to do about it? Hopefully, make sure it doesn't happen again. The Word of God warns us that there will be a great apostasy, a falling away from honesty as we head toward the last days. The choice of listening to the doctrines of devils instead of the truth will be something to consider. 1Tim. 4:1 **The Spirit clearly says that in later times some will abandon the faith and follow deceiving spirits and things taught by demons.**

When there is a polluted river, one needs to go back to the source of the river to find clean water or to the true cleanliness of that river. It is no different in the world today when looking for the true answers to the overwhelming confusion going on in many people's lives. If we go to the source of truth, we find Jesus standing there waiting for us to accept His love and guidance to help us overcome the evil in this hazardous world. John 14:6 **Jesus answered, "I am the way and the truth and the life. No one comes to the Father except through Me.** Jesus said He is the truth or the true story for the rest of us to line our stories with and live in the love God has for us. The Apostle John said there is no falsehood in Jesus. John 7:18b **In Him there is no falsehood.**

Therefore, I will base my life on the true story of Jesus Christ who died on the cross for my sins and gave me eternal life. I do not need to rewrite the history of my sinful past because Jesus is the author and finisher of my faith, and I know He will get the story right. I don't have to cover up the iniquities of my past and minimize the sinfulness I took part in, I can let the Lord's cleansing blood wash away my sins in the fullness of Christ's righteousness. I can confess my sins and be forgiven. I can live the true story God has written for me from the time He first thought of me. Jer. 29:11 **For I know the plans I have for you, declares the LORD, plans to prosper you and not to harm you, to give you a future and a hope.**

From now on, it will be said that Norm's life is based on a true story that was written by God. 1John 5:20 **And we know that the Son of God has come and has given us understanding, so that we may know Him who is true; and we are in Him who is true—in His Son Jesus Christ. He is the true God and eternal life.** It is up to me and all of us to live in the fullness of what has been written in God's Word concerning our lives in Christ and our future with Him. May we live it well! Num. 6:24 **The Lord bless you and keep you; 25 the Lord make his face shine on you and be gracious to you; 26 the Lord turn his face toward you and give you peace.** Thank you, Lord, I love this particular happy ending.

Questions:

Has social media influenced your view of life?

_____

Have you ever fallen for a lie that caused problems in your life?

_____

The Problem With The Problem

Job 22:28 When you make a decision, it will be carried out, and light will shine on your ways.

The problem with the problem is that everyone involved in the problematic situation knows there is a problem but is often overwhelmed by it and has difficulty finding a solution. When the situation becomes dire, people stand around discussing the problem and reinforcing the fact that the problem is bigger than they can manage. There are solutions to all problems, but it seems these people spend more time focusing on the mess. We can all think of family members, acquaintances, or company managers who are in a constant vortex of facing problems that go on and on because these same people are the ones who caused the troubles. These people are always trying to fix a problem they created with a new set of problems that they are instigating. A never-ending cycle of bouncing from one crisis to the other. 2Tim. 3:7 **Ever learning, and never able to come to the knowledge of the truth.**

Years ago when I lived in Queensland Australia, a brother in the Lord asked me for some help. Michael had a brother who did not believe in God nor was friendly toward those who did believe in God. Michael asked me to come out to his brother's papaya plantation to see if I had some ideas to help his brother get out of debt. As well as the papaya plantation, this man also had pigs he was raising for the market, and he was supplementing his farm income by working welding jobs on the side when he could get the work. The reason for all the debt was the considerable mortgage on the farm, the high cost of fertilizer and weed control chemicals, the expensive pig food, and the lack of customers who needed welding done.

We arrived at the farm and I noticed some quarter-inch round, four-foot-high and eight-foot-long metal rod fencing panels leaning against the shed. The owner of this farm described all his woes, and how he could not catch a break because everything was so expensive and no one wanted to help him. I could see why he did not have many customers for welding jobs and why people would be reluctant to help him because he came across as a hard-nosed, 'Don't tell me what to do; I know what I'm doing' type of person.

An idea came to me, and I explained that if he, by welding, made some four-foot high by seven-and-a-half-foot square cages out of the metal round fencing panels, he could put a few pigs in each of the cages and place the cages between the papaya trees that were planted eight feet apart. He and his wife could pick up a cage with one person on opposite sides and move it along to the next square patch of weeds, grass, and ground cover so the pigs could eat and the land would be fertilized simultaneously. This process would naturally enrich the soil thus helping the papaya trees to produce better yield. Michael was so excited about this possible solution that could help his brother bring down some of the costs on the farm. Michael's exuberance was loudly expressed, "Wow, what a great idea because the cost of pig food, fertilizer, and weed killer would go way down and the extra money saved could go toward the mortgage."

Michael's brother then said, "That is the stupidest idea I have ever heard! That will never work, you don't

130

know anything about growing plants." I was not saying that this idea was the be-all to end-all, I was pointing out that with what he had available on his property this might work better than what he was doing. Illumination had been shed on an idea, but the choice to go forward with it was within the property owner's choice to work the plan that could get rid of some problems on the farm. Job 22:28 **When you make a decision, it will be carried out, and light will shine on your ways.** But there it was, as we were driving back home, Michael said, "What an incredible God idea that was, if only my brother would have thought it through, but he has always been a fool and has destroyed everything he has ever put his hands to doing because the problem is that he is the problem." Prov. 27:22 **You can beat a fool half to death and still never beat the foolishness out of him.**

Yes, often the problem with the problem is us. How many times have we rejected the counsel of God and fallen flat on our faces then turned around and asked God why He let us fall? The fact is, had we obeyed we would have solved the complications we found ourselves to be in. Heb. 4:14 **Nothing in all creation is hidden from God's sight. Everything is uncovered and laid bare before the eyes of him to whom we must give account.** King Solomon's son Rehoboam was counselled by the elders of the land to lighten the load of the people, but Rehoboam rejected the counsel. 1Kings 12:8 **But Rehoboam rejected the advice of the elders; instead, he consulted the young men who had grown up with him and served him.** Rehoboam became a problem for the nation as he made the load upon the people heavier than it had to be. 1Kings 12:11

My father laid on you a heavy yoke; I will make it even heavier. My father scourged you with whips; I will scourge you with scorpions. This eventually caused a rebellion and people got hurt.

We see this reenactment of terrible leadership throughout history. Despots, dictators, and tyrants are the cause of so many wars and problems they created. Their solutions are just as problematic, resulting in lost generations of people who end up slaughtered. Self-made problems need solutions. Humility is needed so that the one who caused the mess can humbly ask for help. Jer. 33:3 **Call to Me and I will answer you, and I will tell you great and mighty things, which you do not know.** Looking back to that day at the papaya plantation, all Michael's brother had to do was take a moment to think things through and look at the possible solution available to him at no cost, but his stubborn disposition and anti-God beliefs kept him blind to some simple ideas that could free him from debt. If your problems are mounting up then ask God for help who gives wisdom freely to those who trust and love the Lord. James 1:5 **If you need wisdom, ask our generous God, and he will give it to you. He will not rebuke you for asking.**

Let us not be the reason for the problems, but rather let us be the anointed solution by solving with God's help the problems that come our way. May we all find the grace needed to be victors and not victims of the foolishness running rampant throughout this world. Keep asking God for the answers because He has them.

Question:

Have you ever come up with an amazing solution to a problem you knew was divine inspiration and were shot down anyway?

Get Up And Try Again

Matthew 21:28 What do you think? A man had two sons. He went to the first and said, 'My son, go work in the vineyard today.' 29 He answered and said, I will not: but afterward he repented, and went. 30 Then the man went to the other and said the same thing. 'I will, sir,' he answered, but he didn't go.

Our everyday walk with the Lord is a continual life of choices. What if we make the wrong choice and fall? Through Jesus, we repent and get up again. Our goal is not to run the perfect race, although that would be nice if it could be done, but our purpose is to complete the race that has been set before us through Christ our Lord. Heb. 12:1b **Let us run with patience the race that is set before us, 2a looking to Jesus, the founder and perfecter of our faith.** With Jesus, we can finish what God saw us accomplishing in Him for our lives. Before the foundations of the world, God knew us and set out a plan of redemption that would give us eternal life and purpose in the Kingdom of God. Like the son in Matthew 21:29 who said he would not go to the vineyard to do what his father asked, but then repented and did his father's will, we too have the free will to change our minds and obey our Heavenly Father. We too can get up again after falling on our faces.

The Word says that the righteous man falls but gets up again. Notice, it is a righteous man who fell. It is through the strength of God's righteousness within us that empowers us to repent and get up again. Prov. 24:16 **Though a righteous person falls seven times, he will get up, but the wicked will stumble into ruin.** The wicked will stumble into the mess they keep making because there is no power of God's righteousness at work within their hearts. We who are in Christ have been given the Lord's righteousness to do the will of our God. Praise the Lord for the gift of a righteous life.

The Apostle Paul was always looking ahead to the eternal prize God had for him, and not wallowing in the sins of the past. Phil. 3:13 **Brothers and sisters, I do not regard myself as having taken hold of it yet; but one thing I do: forgetting what lies behind and reaching forward to what lies ahead,** 14 **I press on toward the goal for the prize of the upward call of God in Christ Jesus.** Paul had fallen but got up again. He gives us an example of what the power of salvation can do in the heart of a person who has chosen the Lord Jesus as their Saviour. Even if we fall, we can get up again and look toward the goodness of God for our lives.

I am sure Satan came to Paul with all the accusations concerning the people he had sentenced to death before he encountered Jesus on the road to Damascus. Satan would have kept coming back to Paul with shouts of "You killed them with your religious zeal, and now you say you have wronged no man!" Paul understood the cleansing power and saving grace of the blood of Jesus.

He could declare that he was the righteousness of God through Christ and nothing from his past could change God's mind about the love God had for Paul. That must have burned Satan's cookies to have the accusations he was throwing out at Paul come back and scorch Satan's tongue. Isa. 54:17 **"No weapon that is formed against you will succeed; and you will condemn every tongue that accuses you in judgment. This is the heritage of the servants of the LORD, and their vindication is from Me," declares the LORD.**

Like Paul, we all need to get up again when we fall and make sure we do it right away. The Lord says to come with confident boldness to receive mercy when we need it. Heb.4:16 **Therefore let's approach the throne of grace with confidence, so that we may receive mercy and find grace for help at the time of our need.** The amount of depression and loneliness that is in abundance throughout the world right now is because so many are not getting up again. They have accepted that their failures and inability to find hope of any kind are their lot in life. In many cases, this is the result of living a lawless life and making choices that are contrary to what God says is true and right. Many of them insisted on creating salvation on their terms and now the verdict is in. Their itchy ears and edgy choices have landed them in a lonely place. 2Tim. 4:3 **For the time will come when people will not put up with sound doctrine. Instead, to suit their own desires, they will gather around them a great number of teachers to say what their itching ears want to hear.**

God will not bless your sins of choice, but He will forgive your sins if you repent of them and come home to the Father. The Lord will help you get up again if you want to. Like the son did in Matthew 21:29, you can also do. Matt. 21:29 **He answered and said, I will not: but afterward he repented, and went.** Yes, we can all get up again and continue the race that is ours to finish. We can all say as Paul says, "Forgetting what lies behind and reaching forward to what lies ahead." Our eternity in Christ lies ahead of us and we through Jesus have the confidence in the Lord to keep going because Jesus is the author and finisher of our faith. How good is that?

Question:

What is the most trying event you got back up from after falling?

While We Still Have Breath

Genesis 2:7 And the LORD God formed man of the dust of the ground, and breathed into his nostrils the breath of life; and man became a living soul.

The very first breath that was transferred into Adam's nostrils was God's very own infinite life force making Adam an eternal being. From the first gasp of breathing awareness, Adam experienced eternity, and that eternity had been set in his heart. Eccl. 3:11 **Yet God has made everything beautiful for its own time. He has planted eternity in the human heart, but even so, people cannot see the whole scope of God's work**

from beginning to end. This gift of breath we have been given continues to have God's living life in it, and what we do with the time we have on this earth using these precious breaths counts. We can use them to live a life of selfishness or use them to honour God. We can use them to curse the creator and humanity or we can use them to bless each other and bring joy to God's heart. The choice is ours as to how we are going to breathe while we are on this side of eternity.

I have been asked in the past and asked again recently why I get up so early to post my blogs/articles, and work on the books that I write. Also, this question comes up frequently, "How is it possible to be on the gym floor by 5 a.m. every morning? How early do you have to get up to pull that off?" As many of my readers know, I had a rude awakening a while back when I suffered a stroke because of the obesity I had allowed to take place in my body, plus the poor food choices I was defending as my right to have. The sedentary lifestyle combined with the stroke caused me to be ill for a long time. I had become poverty-stricken in health. Prov. 24:33 **A little sleep, a little slumber, a little folding of the hands to rest, 34 and poverty will come upon you like a robber, and want like an armed man.** Yes, I had allowed my breath of life to be managed by the evil spirit of sloth.

The struggles I had to go through and the effort I had to put in just to be able to catch my breath during that first year of recovery, clearly demonstrated to me that I had misused and mismanaged the health of my body. Like so many people, I had forgotten that the breath God gave me was a gift and that I was the temple of the Holy Spirit. 1Cor. 6:19 **Don't you realize that your body is the temple of the Holy Spirit, who lives**

in you and was given to you by God? You do not belong to yourself. That was it. I had forgotten I did not belong to myself; I belonged to the Lord, who paid for me in full with His sacrifice on the cross.

The transfer of eternal life and the privilege of God's breath in my nostrils is a miracle indeed. To this day, I am still fighting to maintain my health, redeem the time that was given to me, and be a trustworthy steward of the life God gave me. Many of us put these commitments off to a place called *I'll get around to it,* but like so many we find ourselves heading into the second half or fourth quarter of our lives and the realization of our capability to rise to life's challenges leaves us breathless. Psalm 90:12 **So teach us to number our days, that we may present to You a heart of wisdom.**

Recently, the news of friends whose premature deaths and some who have ended up with terrible diseases has rattled my consciousness, and the news of friends losing limbs and mobility to diabetes caused me to double down on my commitments to taking care of the life I have left. The effort I am giving to take care of my temple does not mean I will live any longer than others, but hopefully it means I will have a quality of life that will continue till the number of my days drops from the hand of my God. Job 14:5 **Our time on earth is brief; the number of our days is already decided by you.** Therefore, while I have breath I will use it to the best of my ability to do the things God expects of me. God asks that we love one another, pray for each other, and be a brother or sister who can walk in God's anointing to bring healing that is needed in this harsh and lost world. Matt. 5:9 **Blessed are the peacemakers, for they will be called sons of God.**

While we still have time, let us get on with what God has sown in our hearts to do. Stop putting it off when it is in your power to get on with it. Empty declarations of "I'll get on that diet someday, or soon I will start going to the gym again and lose this extra eighty pounds" are just empty words. Lies of "I'll get out of this toxic relationship any day now, and I will spend more time in prayer once I get through all the dilemmas in my life" are all wasted breaths. This type of slothful rhetoric allows death to wait at the door of our lives so that we may be consumed with lying to ourselves. Let us stop and smell the holy aroma God has granted us to walk in and be the blessing we were created to be.

Question:

What have you been putting off that you know you need to get to it fast?

_____

That Day!

Luke 21:34 Be on your guard, so that your minds are not dulled from carousing, drunkenness, and worries of life, or that day will come on you unexpectedly.

1Thessalonians 5:2 **For you yourselves know full well that the day of the Lord will come just like a thief in the night.** This is not a subject people want to think about or face, and yet the Scripture says "We know full well that day is coming." The day of the Lord will come. That day has an appointed calendar date and will happen regardless of one's belief concerning it. Some have mocked the second coming of Jesus, but be assured, that day will come and the mockers will face the truth of their sarcastic hearts. 2Pet. 3:3 **Above all, be aware of this: Scoffers will come in the last days scoffing and following their own evil desires, 4 saying, "Where is His 'coming' that He promised? Ever since our ancestors fell asleep, all things continue as they have been since the beginning of creation."**

The ease of letting our guards down and going along with the momentum of everyday life and agreeing with those who dictate the secular terms of life is a path to becoming anesthetized in our souls. This can result in a quiet submission to the world's offerings causing a dullness of spirit. Heb. 5:11 **Concerning this we have much to say, and it is hard to explain, since you have become dull and sluggish in [your spiritual] hearing and disinclined to listen.** We need to stay alert to what the Holy Spirit is saying to our hearts and not disregard the warnings that were declared for the times we are living in.

The people who lived during the pre-diluvian judgment mocked what Noah was doing and the warnings that a day of judgment was coming. It is believed among scholars that the building of the ark and warnings to those people lasted about a hundred and twenty years before the cataclysmic event erupted. Then a final countdown was given to Noah: in seven days the flood would begin. What a pronouncement to have heard and get one's heart ready to go through. Imagine hearing that in seven days— in one week— the world-changing judgment and flood would begin. Suddenly, that day was upon them. Gen. 7:4 **Seven days from now I will send rain on the earth for forty days and forty nights, and I will wipe from the face of the earth every living creature I have made.**

The closest generalization to the date recorded of the great flood was the seventeenth of MarCheshvan (sometimes called Cheshvan), the second month of the Jewish calendar. Gen. 7:11 **In the six hundredth year of Noah's life, in the second month, on the seventeenth day of the month, on this day all the fountains of the great deep split open, and the floodgates of the sky were opened.** The words, "On this day all the fountains of the great deep split open." These words of judgment came to pass, and that calendar date went down in history as the most destructive day ever to come upon the human race. Our minds cannot begin to imagine the sound of the earth cracking open like many hydro dams busting out all at once and the water creating an intense roaring noise, plus the groans of all living things gasping for the last breath of life. The horror is too much to take in and maybe this is why many do not want to think of the next judgment to take place on earth.

These people were going about their business as the Scriptures say in Luke 17:26 **Just as it was in the days of Noah, so it will be in the days of the Son of Man: 27 People went on eating, drinking, marrying and being given in marriage until the day Noah boarded the ark, and the flood came and destroyed them all.** The question we need to answer in our hearts is, "Are we doing the same thing these people were doing before the flood?" Are we just filling in time, or doing our best not to become mockers of the righteous and those who desire Godliness on earth? Are we maintaining our hearts in the forthrightness of the Lord's love and doing our best to live the way God has asked us to? Are we paying attention to the times we are in? Hopefully, we are those who have been trying to share the love of God on this lost earth despite all the wrong that is now commonplace. We need to be reminded of God's warnings and take them to heart. The days are short and we would be wise not to get caught up or invested in what the world is hell bent on doing.

The Lord gives us a joyful clue as to what we should be doing when we see these terrible events taking place as that day approaches. Luke 21:28 **Now when these things begin to take place, straighten up and raise your heads, because your redemption is drawing near**. Wow, the Lord said to straighten up and raise your head. No hang-dog attitudes toward the mess going on. Rather, a command to raise our heads toward heaven and while we are doing that, we might as well pray for the people who are living through this mess. God still answers prayer and we have been admonished to keep praying till the Lord returns. Col. 4:2 **Continue earnestly in prayer, being vigilant in it with thanksgiving**. Yes, Saints, that day when the Lord returns will be a calendar event. Let us prepare our hearts to meet Him and be a blessing while we wait for that day. Yes, Lord Jesus come!

Questions:

Is the day of the Lord an important day on your eternal calendar?

_____

What is one question you want answered when you meet the Lord face to face?

_____

Finish Strong

Jeremiah 12:5 If you have run with the footmen, and they have wearied you, then how can you contend with horses? And if in the land of peace, in which you trusted, they wearied you, then how will you do in the floodplain of the Jordan?

Finish strong, or however you want to say it, "Finish strong, finish hard, or finish right." Do your best to finish the race God has placed you in with the life He has given you. I caught myself looking at the clock at the gym and wondering how much time I had left to complete my workout. I quickly reprimanded myself for looking for an easy finish. I had to say out loud, "Come on Norm, finish strong!" When I catch myself making up excuses for being a slacker in things that need to get done, I often think of Jeremiah's words, "If you have run with the footmen, and they have wearied you, then how can you contend with horses?" How true is that? If

I can't do the things that I need to do daily, what am I going to do if times get really hard?

If I can't pray and spend time with God when the days are good, how will I ask for help during a frantic panic when the world is crashing around me? If I cannot control my eating habits and make sure I am exercising regularly, how will I find the courage and willpower to work out and eat properly when a diagnosis of multiple deadly conditions comes rushing at me like an armed bandit to take over my existence? How can I finish strong when all my choices are weak and undisciplined wishful thinking? Prov. 14:23 **All hard work brings a profit, but mere talk leads only to poverty.**

We hear people say these wishful things all the time. I wish I could get up early and spend time with the Lord. I wish I could get to work on time. I wish I could push away from the table when I am full. Prov. 13:4 **A sluggard's appetite is never filled, but the desires of the diligent are fully satisfied.** I wish I would get off my lazy butt and do what needs to be done. On and on the wishing goes. To be able to finish strong, we need to become strong in the areas of life where God has sown inspirational tenacity within us to accomplish what we were created to fulfill. Prov. 23:7a **For as he thinks within himself, so he is.** We need to break through the walls of laziness that everyone has experienced throughout their lives. Not everyone is hard-wired to take on every challenge that comes their way. Some will need to apply much more effort than others just to accomplish small tasks. That is fine, as long as you finish strong and go on to the next Godly life-changing lesson for living in Christ's righteousness.

For some, making their bed before they leave home

may be the Goliath they need to conquer, and for others, it may be finishing their doctorate in the field of learning that burns in their hearts. Nevertheless, whatever magnitude the task is, finishing strong will help determine the character of heart one has in life. I was asked, what if I had a very short time to live, and the book I was writing would not get finished? I said, "I reckon I would write faster." Not trying to be a wise guy, but these hypothetical questions of *What if* do not matter when you are living your best life to the fullest and are doing the best you can with what the Lord has given you. Besides, it is God who determines what we do and eventually accomplish. Yes, we are willing participants in the plan God has for us, therefore, worrying about what gets finished in our lives is His problem. I say this reverently because God has the number of our days in His hands. Our job or raison d'etre is to go forth in Christ's righteousness and finish the race set before us.

I am sure the Apostle Paul could have done much more had he not been killed during Nero's reign of persecution towards the Christians. He knew his time was short. Paul declares that he will finish strong and that there will be a blessed reward at the end of it all. 2Tim. 4:6 **For I am already being poured out like a drink offering, and the time for my departure is near. 7 I have fought the good fight, I have finished the race, I have kept the faith.** He finished his race even though he had the knowledge and capacity to have done much more. My point is that Paul finished strong, and we are blessed because of it. We have his letters to the church, which help direct and instruct us to live in Christ's righteousness.

Whatever the trials and tribulations that show up

on our road to eternity are, they can be conquered with the help and guidance of the Holy Spirit. The thing that is often missing in Christian's lives is the will within a person to move ahead when the Spirit of God is prodding them along. Many become weary and tired because they do not do the small things their faith requires to grow. Complacency becomes a default setting in the heart, and insipidness becomes the fruit of their day-to-day existence. The Word expressly warns us not to give up on what God has inspired us to sow into. Gal. 6:9 **And let us not grow weary of doing good, for in due season we will reap, if we do not give up**. If God has given us a vision, then God will give us the means to fulfill it and finish strong.

Questions:

What legacy do you want to leave to celebrate the fact that you had been a resident of earth and God's great plan?

_____

If you could talk to your younger self, what advice would you give that wonderful person?

_____

Norm-Isms

Let God bug you!

God and you are the majority

Don't sell yourself short when you are tall in your heart. Know your worth.

Part Four
What Is Your Discipline?

I am a person who needs discipline to function. Without it, I am an accident waiting to happen. I need the Lord's discipline because His Word says so and I know for a fact that I can do nothing significant without it. If we do not learn to discipline our lives then life will bring a discipline much harder than is reasonable. I do not need to go to prison to know that the way of a transgressor is hard, and a lack of discipline leads to dumb choices. When I am asked, "What is your discipline?" My answer is simple, "Whatever God is leading me into, is the discipline of the moment." Proverbs 12:1 **Whoever loves discipline loves knowledge, but he who hates reproof is stupid.**

What Is Your Discipline?

1Corinthians 9:27 But I discipline my body and keep it under control, lest after preaching to others I myself should be disqualified.

The Apostle Paul makes it clear that we need to apply discipline to our lives so that we live within the fullness of God's grace that has been lavished upon our lives through Christ. Discipline is not something someone else can give us, we need to grow into it and allow the discipline to develop our character. What disciplines do you have working in your life right now? What knowledge have you acquired that came to you because you love discipline? Prov. 12:1 **Whoever loves discipline loves knowledge, but he who hates reproof is stupid.** Have you mastered a discipline that has brought a quality of life to your soul, or, as the proverb indicates, have you become a stupid person because you cannot be reproved? I am not the one saying anyone is stupid, I am reading the Proverb in its context, and it says if I hate the reproval of God's discipline, then I will become a stupid person.

The Word of the Lord is filled with exhortations and admonitions to apply different disciplines to our lives. James says that if we could discipline our tongues, we would be able to control many other aspects of our lives. James 3:2 **Indeed, we all make many mistakes. For if we could control our tongues, we would be perfect and could also control ourselves in every other way.** The issue is if we do not learn to discipline, control, or rein in our tongues, then the effects of what we say that is contrary to God's will can come back and destroy everything we have been trying to build. Eccl. 5:6 **Don't let your mouth make you sin. And don't defend yourself by telling the Temple messenger that the promise you made was a mistake. That would make God angry, and he might wipe out everything you have achieved.**

We are to be disciplined when we sit down to negotiate for the things needed in life. Don't just sign away your life because you want the purchase so badly. Prov. 23:1 **While dining with a ruler, pay attention to what is put before you. 2 And put a knife to your throat if you are given to gluttony. 3 Do not desire his delicacies, for they are deceptive food.** Control your impulses, and use the discipline of God's Word to redirect your cravings. What is your discipline, and where are you exercising it? Where are you developing the gifts given to you by God? Will we be able to give our Lord a return on the giftings we have received? Luke 19:15 **"He was made king, however, and returned home. Then he sent for the servants to whom he had given the money, in order to find out what they had gained with it.** 16 **"The first one came and said, 'Sir, your mina has earned ten more.'** 17 **"'Well done, my good servant!' his master replied. 'Because you have been trustworthy in a very small matter, take charge of ten cities.'** Take charge of the responsibility God has given you, and become disciplined because your next task of faith will need the directional help from God.

We are to be disciplined in our work and not just give lip service to those who are expecting quality results from our lives. Eph. 6:5 **Bondservants, be obedient to those who are your earthly masters, with respect for authority, and with a sincere heart seeking to please them, as service to Christ—** 6 **not in the way of eye-service working only when someone is watching you and only to please men, but as slaves of Christ, doing the will of God from your heart.** If we cannot get up and get ready for the work of the day, then we will falter when God asks us to do a hard thing. If we are not disciplined in the service of what God has given us to do, then we will not be faithful when the Lord asks us to step up to greater maturity and be a blessing to someone we feel does not deserve it. Instead of ministering from God's heart, we will end up judging from our hearts.

Job 36:10 **He opens also their ear to discipline, and commands that they return from iniquity.** The way back from sin and iniquity can be a hard road to walk upon if we do not have the leading of the Holy Spirit. Our willingness to return to the Love of the Father will take the dedication of a committed person to fulfill what God is asking of us. Once we have made the decision to repent and submit to the guidance of our Lord, it will take the wisdom and knowledge of God's Word to walk circumspectly before Him. If we want to live in the shadow of the Almighty and bask in His surrounding love, then we need to be disciplined in heart and cleansed through the blood of Jesus. Psalm 91:1 **He who dwells in the shelter of the Most High will abide in the shadow of the Almighty.**

The question remains: What is your discipline? My discipline is what God helps me control through His grace, love, and strength so that I do not disqualify myself. 1Cor. 9:27 **But I discipline my body and keep it under control, lest after preaching to others I myself should be disqualified.** How does one develop this discipline? We learn to love the disciplines in our life and we reap the knowledge of God. Prov. 12:1a **Whoever loves discipline loves knowledge.** If our hearts are to know Him, then we must become hearers of His Word, and obedient to respond to His leading. The love of God for each one of us is never in doubt. However, friendship and relationship with our Heavenly Father can only come through Jesus Christ the Lord, and it is through His loving discipline in our lives that we enjoy His eternal presence within our hearts. Our discipline is being loved and loving God. May we all become skilled at it.

Everything Costs

2Samuel 24:24 But the king said to Araunah, "No, but I will buy it from you for a price. I will not offer burnt offerings to the LORD my God that cost me nothing." So David bought the threshing floor and the oxen for fifty shekels of silver.

It does not matter where you go or what you do. The fact is, everything costs and will eventually require payment from our lives. Whether we are acquiring substances for our daily needs or the purchase of goods and services, everything costs us time, money, and energy. Somewhere and somehow we will pay the price of life. There is a full supply of what we need on earth, but the energy and willpower to take possession of it and retain what we are after will cost us. Even a criminal knows there is a crime cost when the criminal ends up in jail. They pay for their lives with time served and labour performed until the social debt is paid for. Matt. 18:34 **And in anger his master delivered him to the jailers, until he should pay all his debt**. If you own a home, there are costs to maintain it and keep it sound and structurally safe. If you own a vehicle, there are a variety of costs that come with owning that vehicle. If you run or walk, the soles of your shoes will eventually need replacing and there will be a need to pay for another pair. Yes, everything in life costs us something.

There is a saying among Christians that rings true. "Salvation is free, but discipleship will cost your life." Jesus indicated that we need to count the cost of our decision if we were to follow Him. Luke 14:28 **For**

which of you, desiring to build a tower, does not
first, having sat down, count the cost, whether he
has enough for its completion?** Even though there is
an eternal blessing in accepting Jesus as our Lord, the
choice to follow Him can cost us friends, family members,
and even employment. The Lord said that if the world
hated Him, they would hate His followers as well, and
there would be an emotional levy to serving the Lord.
In some parts of the world, the price of following Jesus
is their lives or the lives of their loved ones. Heb. 11:37
**Some died by stoning, some were sawed in half, and
others were killed with the sword. Some went about
wearing skins of sheep and goats, destitute and
oppressed and mistreated.**

Anyone who has served the Lord has felt the
emotional weight and cost when a spouse mentions that
God is getting more attention than they are. When the
minister's children say that other fathers are better to their
children because they get to go and do other things that
are not ministry-related. There is a toll to making sure
that as Christians we are not involved with the workings
of evil. 1Thes. 5:22 **Abstain from all appearance of
evil**. The Missionary who has lost their spouse, child,
or health while taking care of God's business on the
mission field can become overwhelmed by the tally of
sacrificial submissions Jesus is asking of them. Living in
the presence of the Lord will cost our flesh dearly.

We must understand that when Jesus asks us to walk
with Him, our lives now belong to Him. We are obliged
within our souls to hand over the total value we have
placed upon our lives and be willing to fulfil the call
God has placed upon us. 2Sam. 24:24 **But the king said
to Araunah, "No, but I will buy it from you for a**

price. I will not offer burnt offerings to the LORD my God that cost me nothing." So David bought the threshing floor and the oxen for fifty shekels of silver. David understood that personal sacrifice was going to be needed when serving and walking with the Lord. Even a sacrifice of praise has a tariff connected to it. The simple fact is that if it is a sacrifice of praise, then the praise comes from a place of difficulty within our hearts. Keeping our word to God often requires a sacrifice on our part which will extract a choice of will.

The Lord understands the dedication of heart and the total cost we feel when handing our lives over to His Lordship. This is why He gives us His grace to be able to do it. Jesus submitted every part of His life to His Heavenly Father. This same grace and anointing reside within each one of us, but as David expressed when sacrificing to the Lord, we have to want to pay that significant price. Christ is faithful and will always keep His word toward us, even if we break our vows and promises made to Him. 2Tim. 2:13 **If we are faithless, He remains faithful, for He is not able to deny Himself.** It is this faithfulness that Jesus has toward us that gives us strength to rise and give ourselves over to His will.

Sin cost Jesus everything. We owed a debt we could not pay. The eternal price for our souls to be made whole again could not have been bought by anyone except Jesus. The Lord paid for our sins in full, and the cost of our sins was placed upon the Son of God as He was nailed to the cross of pain and torture. Historically and to this day, sin has cost all humanity countless amounts of pain and suffering that could never be paid for within a billion lifetimes. Our souls were bought with the loving grace and gift of God's goodness that was lavished on us through the sacrifice of Jesus Christ the Lord. Jesus counted the cost and paid it. Let us enjoy the blessing of being redeemed by what Jesus did for us. Yes, everything costs, but our Redeemer lives and we have been made free because of His love.

Questions:

How has the reality of Christianity differed from the cost you thought it would be?

_____

Jesus paid our debt in full. Have you accepted that gift, or do you struggle to earn it?

_____

My Toolbox

2 Corinthians 10:4 For the weapons of our warfare are not carnal but mighty in God for pulling down strongholds, 5 casting down arguments and every high thing that exalts itself against the knowledge of God, bringing every thought into captivity to the obedience of Christ.

I am like everyone else in the body of Christ. I have been cleansed by the soul-saving sacrifice of Jesus Christ and given His grace through His gift of righteousness. My Heavenly Father has also supplied me, as He has everyone in His kingdom, with a toolbox full of enhanced tools that we can use to help build His realm and tear down the structures of darkness. The tools that the Lord has made available to us can be used to heal the brokenhearted, set free those who have become captives by the vices of this world, and help all mankind be reconciled with each other and God because this is the will of God. 2Cor. 5:18 **All this is from God, who through Christ reconciled us to himself and gave us the ministry of reconciliation**. The key is that all the work we do is through and because of what Jesus has done for us.

Our tools are diversified and accurately crafted to fulfill the assignment God has given us within His kingdom. Our ministry tools can destroy the works and hostility the kingdom of darkness uses against God's children. We have been given the blood of Jesus and His Word to strengthen our hearts and our resolve in the faith so that we are courageous when overcoming the plans Satan has developed against our lives. Rev. 12:11 **And they have overcome him by reason of the blood of the Lamb, and by reason of the word of their testimony; and they have not loved their life unto death**. We are encouraged by God to develop our faith and use the authority we have been given in Christ to pull down the strongholds that the enemy of our souls has crafted against us. We are to do this while wearing the armour of God so that we can stand against the tricks of the enemy. The Lord has also given us the Holy Spirit to take care of ourselves and each other's needs in God's Kingdom where we are rightful citizens.

Similarly, to owning the tools in our toolbox to fix what needs to be repaired around the house, yard, car, and so on, we have tools that work in the kingdom of God. The Lord's anointing, truth, righteousness, and grace will help us get the job done that we have been created to fulfill. These heavenly and holy tools are available to us as we prayerfully use them. We are yoked to the Lord Jesus and there is nothing we cannot accomplish if we are in step with the Lord. The key is learning to stay in step with His plan and His guidance, then the tools in our heavenly toolbox work and fit the job well.

Someone might say, "I do not know how to use any tools. I can't even swing a hammer without hurting myself or anyone within fifty yards of me." This may be the facts at this time, but the truth is, you can learn how to swing that hammer to become productive and a skilled user. We need to be willing to learn how to use what God has given us and not judge what the Lord has put within our hands to do His work. This was God's question when He asked Moses, "What is in your hand?" Ex. 4:2 **Then the LORD asked him, "What is that in your hand?" "A shepherd's staff," Moses replied**. The conversation gets intense at this point because, with that staff that Moses was familiar with, God says that Moses will deliver a nation out of captivity. Ex. 4:17 **And take your shepherd's staff with you, and use it to perform the miraculous signs I have shown you**. How had something that Moses used every day become the tool to deliver a nation? Only God can work the miracle needed with what we have at the moment.

Moses became skilled at using the tool God gave him. That rod was used to lead the nation, part the waters of the Red Sea, win the war against the Amalekites, and bring water out of a rock to quench the thirst of man and beast. If God says to you, "What is in your hand or what is in your house," do not shy away or be embarrassed from answering with the little that might be there. 2Kings 4:2 **Elisha replied to her, "How can I help you? Tell me, what do you have in your house?" "Your servant has nothing there at all," she said, "except a small jar of olive oil."** Lift your head to your Lord and say, "All I have is a little jar," and see what God can do with it.

Moses honed his skills with the rod and delivered a nation. The widow became a connoisseur of oil and saved her family. David was made king because he swung a rock-loaded sling and hit the mark that would change history. The Apostles changed the world because they were filled with the Holy Spirit. What have you looked upon in your toolbox that you have treated as not that valuable? In my life, I have seen the Lord turn my illiteracy into a tool of writing that helps people reason and find comfort in the Word of God. We all need to become better skilled with the tools available to us that are in our toolbox for the working and building of the Kingdom in which God has placed us.

We cannot discount what God has given us by comparing it with others and the tools that others have learned to use efficiently. We all need to work in His Kingdom and use what we have so that when we become skilled at using a particular tool, the Lord gives us another one to learn how to use for His purposes in this life. May we all become workmen not ashamed of what we have and who we are in Christ. 2Tim. 2:15 **Be diligent to present yourself approved to God, a worker who does not need to be ashamed, rightly dividing the word of truth.**

Question:

What are your skills and how do you use them to help build the kingdom of your God?

This Is! I Will!

Psalm 118:24 This is the day the LORD has made; We will rejoice and be glad in it.

I can personalize the above Scripture to say "I will rejoice and be glad." I choose to rejoice, be a blessing, and be glad that God loves me, no matter what *This Day* may hold. The facts of the day's events we face are the events we must go through because the day is what it is. We can prepare for certain occurrences like earthquakes, tsunamis, and tornados, but these catastrophic incidents are beyond our control. We cannot change a day's events but determine how we will walk during the day's difficulties that are happening around us. Psalm 118:24 **This is the day the LORD has made; We will rejoice and be glad in it.** Our attitude toward what we face will help us overcome overwhelming odds. On the other hand, the day that the Lord has made may bring some of the most cherished, happy, and loving events we have ever experienced. On all counts of life's happenings, we choose how to respond to the gift of life that God gave us.

Everyone has had to confront and live through the day that is at hand. Some of the horrific and terrifying things that have taken place throughout history have all taken place on the day that the Lord had made, and some of the greatest victories, love stories, and miraculous comebacks took place on the same created days. It was a terrible day when the announcement of the Second World War hit the newspaper headlines, and It was a wonderful day when the same newspapers read *The War Is Over*! It was a heartbreaking day when you were told you had cancer, but it was a smile from ear to ear day when you were told that you had beaten it. Deut. 30:19 **Today I have given you the choice between life and death, between blessings and curses. Now I call on heaven and earth to witness the choice you make. Oh, that you would choose life, so that you and your descendants might live!**

This is the day the Lord has made and I will be what God expects of me on this day. This is what it is, and we will respond through the grace of our God. The day that I suffered a stroke was the day that the Lord had made, and the day I covenanted with the Lord to do all that I could to change the course of my health, was also a day of the Lord. The day I found out that my son was addicted to heroin was a day of the Lord that I wish I could forget. The day that my son was set free from all addiction and the effects of enslavement was also a day of the Lord that I remember fondly. There is a choice of whether we will rejoice in the day or we will curse the day we are in. The choice is not easy to be made but it is a choice that must be made because we will end up with the results of our choice.

In the story of Job, there is every kind of emotional turmoil taking place in this recorded account of Job's life. Everything was going well for Job until one day, everything was destroyed. From the total loss of positions to the death of family members, Job suffered a loss of epic proportions. As hard as it sounds, Job in effect rejoiced in the day that was made when he said, Job 1:21 **And he said, "Naked I came from my mother's womb, and naked shall I return. The LORD gave, and the LORD has taken away; blessed be the name of the LORD."** In the misery of the day's events, Job had not chosen to curse the day nor blame God. Job 1:22 **In all of this, Job did not sin by blaming God.**

There was another day when the devil brought undue pressure into Job's life by causing boils to break out all over his body. The excruciating pain became unbearable and after many days Job cursed the day he was born. Job 3:1 **After this, Job opened his mouth and cursed the day of his birth.** The psychological attack on Jobs's character by his friends would have been hard to hear and try to reason through. Nothing was working out for Job. He eventually had a heart-to-heart with God. The Lord pointed out that Job's hardship was real but greater things were going on around him that were unexplainable. Therefore, Job responded with a repentant heart and declared Job 42:3 **You said to me 'Who is this that darkens and obscures counsel by words without knowledge?' Therefore I now see I have rashly uttered that which I did not understand, Things too wonderful for me, which I did not know.** In effect, Job said, "This is God's day, and I will be glad in God."

Sometimes we need to stop fighting what God is doing in the day we are in and declare, "This is the day God created, and I will live to the fullness within it!" There may be times that we will go through a Job experience of unfairness (as we perceive what is fair in life) and will need to choose the revelatory Word of God to get us through the hard times. But as the Psalmist said, Psalm 30:5b **Weeping may tarry for the night, but joy comes with the morning**. Yes, praise God, because we eventually come through the storms of life, and find the strength to seize the day that the Lord has made for our growth and victory. Therefore, let the day of the Lord be our favourite time for living.

Questions:

Does the joy of the Lord come easily to you, or do you need to press in and rejoice by faith?

_____

What has been your hardest battle in your Christian walk so far?

_____

Keeping Your Promise In The Darkness

Luke 23:42 Then he said, "Jesus, remember me when you come into your kingdom." 43 Jesus answered him, "Truly I tell you, today you will be with me in paradise."

In the raw and brutal scene taking place on the

cross, the onlookers who witnessed the crucifixion of Christ had no idea they were watching the very act of redemption unfolding before their eyes. The crucifixion of Jesus for the salvation of our souls was never more apparent than when the thief being crucified with Christ asked to be remembered in the Lord's kingdom. This happened while Jesus was in the grips of the greatest darkness He had ever lived through. The symbolization that this event taught was profound. The thieves were the bottom feeders of society and the Lord was the perfection of God's love and anointing. On the hill of sorrow, they were being crucified next to each other upon cruel crosses implemented by the darkness of man's imagination. Without understanding, as the crowd watched the vicious treatment of Jesus, they were looking at their redemption taking place and the baptism some of them would become part of. Rom. 6:3 **Do you not know that all of us who have been baptized into Christ Jesus were baptized into his death?**

The crucifixion that was happening in front of everyone's eyes, was a living lesson that demonstrated God's love for those who would receive Christ's sacrifice. Rom. 5:8 **But God showed his great love for us by sending Christ to die for us while we were still sinners.** How confusing and mind-bending it must have been for those watching and hearing the sounds of pitiful keening and sobs of human darkness, and not understanding that God was redeeming their lives as a result of the suffering Jesus was experiencing. They were witnessing the gruesome torture of the cross, and could not read into the event that Jesus was fulfilling the redemption for mankind. The love of God for all man was taking place through this sacrificial offering that

Jesus made of Himself for the propitiation of our sins.

The eternal reason for Jesus coming to earth to save us from our sins and iniquities took place in front of all during the crucifixion. The events leading to the cross represented Jesus taking our place on that cross. The criminal Barabas was supposed to be on the cross next to the thieves that day. However, Jesus in reality, took Barabas' place on that cross because the crowd's choice of who would be crucified between Jesus and Barabas was made through their insistent screaming, "Crucify Him, crucify Him." Jesus took Barabas' and our place on that cross for the punishment we deserved for our sins. In the darkness, as Jesus hung on the cross of shame, the thieves cursed Jesus and mocked His goodness which is what we have done throughout our lives by the hypocrisies we have chosen to live in. We are as guilty as Barabas was, but Jesus took our place.

In the darkness taking place on Calvary, the onlookers were seeing that God the Father was keeping His promise to mankind by providing a once-and-for-all eternal sacrifice for the remission of sins. In that gloom, the public witnessed Jesus keeping His promise to mankind as the lamb of God who takes away the world's sins. In the absence of light that came upon the land in the sixth hour until the ninth hour the Holy Spirit showed mankind what their sins had done to all creation. Luke 23:44 **And now it was about the sixth hour, and darkness came over the whole land until the ninth hour.** They were in a state of constant and perpetual blackness and would need this horrific sacrifice to deliver them forever from the dark that their souls were capable of creating. The Godhead kept their promise to give mankind a new heart that would be receptive to God.

There were two kinds of darkness at work on Calvary that day. There was the shadowiness that we are accustomed to, which the thieves lived in and brought to people's lives because of the dark deeds and choices they made in life, plus there was the total infinite darkness of God's judgment that Jesus was immersed in while He hung in shame. This visual demonstration of what the cross was fulfilling for mankind could be seen but not understood until the resurrection. This is why the blabbering of the haters who claimed that if Jesus came down from the cross, they would believe. This was just more nonsense that a sinful heart invents to rationalize and justify one's sinful choices. They would not have believed anything Jesus did in the natural at that point because they were already aware of the incredible miracles the Lord had created while He walked amongst them. John 21:25 **Jesus did many other things as well. If every one of them were written down, I suppose that even the whole world would not have room for the books that would be written.**

These same Jesus haters are with us today and they are saying the same thing as they did then. Those of us who are in Christ have the capacity because of what Jesus did for us. To remain faithful and keep our promises in the darkness that is visible on all sides of life today. Jesus took our place on the cursed cross so that we would be His hand extended in this world and bring the blessings of the Holy to mankind. The strength and maturity needed to keep our promise when everything around us is covered in the blackness of the dark will be given to us by the Holy Spirit who will guide us into all truth. John 16:13 **But when He, the Spirit of truth, shall come, He will guide you into all the truth. For He will not speak**

165

from Himself, but whatever He may hear, He will speak. And He will declare to you the things coming.

The Lord has given us every tool and fortification in the spirit needed to overcome the wickedness that comes against us. We are admonished to put on the whole armour of God. We are asked to pray with all manner of prayers. We are advised to resist the devil and he will flee. We are led by the Spirit of God to think and meditate on the goodness of God and while we are doing these things, Jesus is interceding for us before our Heavenly Father so that we remain faithful and keep our promises in the darkness that is in the world. Oh, how true it is that we are the light of the world and the salt of the earth. Jesus was faithful to the thief and kept His promise amid His crucifixion. This same Lord is asking us to stay strong in the power of the Holy Spirit and be a light in this world of death while becoming the blessing we were created to be in Christ. Thank you, Lord, that we can do all things through Christ who strengthens us and loves us now and forevermore.

Questions:

Have you given a promise to someone or to God that you have not kept?

_____

What promise made to you, do you wish had been kept and lived up to?

_____

Knowing How To Show Up

2Kings 6:16 He said, "Do not be afraid, for those who are with us are more than those who are with them."**17** Then Elisha prayed and said, "O LORD, please open his eyes that he may see." So the LORD opened the eyes of the young man, and he saw, and behold, the mountain was full of horses and chariots of fire all around Elisha.

Our Heavenly Father knows how to show up when we are in need. He can change the circumstances of a terrible situation in a millisecond. The Lord knows how to show up and make a difference. When Jesus went to an event or encountered lives who needed a miraculous intervention, changes came about because Jesus was there and He had shown up in the power of God. Jesus came to the tomb where Lazarus was lying dead and wrapped in grave cloth while the family members were grieving the pain of loss. Even though Lazarus had been dead for four days Jesus showed up on time to make a difference in the lives of those at the gravesite. John 11:43 **After Jesus had said this, He called out in a loud voice, "Lazarus, come out!"** What a miraculous turn of events from death to life, from being a stench to a sweet savour blessing to all. When God does something on our behalf it is done right and in full measure, nothing lacking.

Job was a man who showed up for those who needed help. Job 4:3 **Indeed, you have instructed many and have strengthened weak hands. 4 Your words have steadied the one who was stumbling and braced the**

knees that were buckling. Job knew how to make a difference in someone's life and take care of the situation that needed attending to as he encountered the problem. Job 29:12 **For I rescued the poor man who cried out for help, and the fatherless child who had no one to support him**. Job did not wait for a committee to approve what he saw needing attention; he did what needed doing. Job did what the proverb asks us all to do: to be a voice and a helper to the voiceless. Prov. 31:8 **Open your mouth for the mute, For the rights of all who are unfortunate and defenceless; 9 Open your mouth, judge righteously, And administer justice for the afflicted and needy**.

There is a lack of decision-making ability in society these days. Many stop to take pictures and record the problem, the skirmish, or the devastation taking place in front of their mobile devices, but not many are stepping forward to help fix the problem or assist practically. Some are afraid to step forward because they might get sued for something that goes wrong while trying to help someone in danger. Many just do not know what to do, and others don't care as they feel they have enough problems of their own. Knowing how to show up in someone's life has become harder to do because the issues of life have become so diverse and confusing. Imagine, lending a hand has become confusing and something that is no longer a natural occurrence.

This was not the case when Abram heard that his nephew Lot had been taken captive. Abram armed his men, showed up and took care of the problem. Gen. 14:14 **When Abram heard that his nephew Lot had been captured, he armed and led out his trained men, born in his own house, numbering three**

hundred and eighteen, and went in pursuit as far north as Dan. Nothing is stopping us from praying for any problem that is big or small that we come across on our daily walk. One of the names of God is *The Lord of the Breakthrough.* 2Sam. 5:20 **So David came to Baal-perazim, and he defeated them there, and said, "The LORD has broken through my enemies before me, like a breakthrough of water." So he named that place Baal-perazim master of breakthroughs.** Maybe we do not know what to do in a particular situation, however, we can pray and ask the Lord of Glory to show up for the people in need of deliverance and break through the mess that has surrounded them.

We can ask God to bring about the help a person needs and ask Him to show us how we can help if need be. It only takes spiritual will in the same way it takes political will to get things done that bring better living conditions for the citizens of a country or town. There is no room for an attitude of languor in the Christian walk. We are all called to the ministry of reconciliation. 2Cor. 5:18 **All this is from God, who reconciled us to Himself through Christ and gave us the ministry of reconciliation: 19 that God was reconciling the world to Himself in Christ, not counting men's trespasses against them. And He has committed to us the message of reconciliation.** The Lord admonishes us to be reconciled to God and one another. The first step in being a blessing to those in your life is to be reconciled to God. How can we show up for a difficult situation if we are not faithful to show up for the small and attainable things God asks of us?

Knowing how to be available as one of God's family members takes practice and willpower on our behalf. We need to be intentional, available, and malleable to the will of God as we live our lives in Christ and bring His peace into this world. The closer we get to knowing the will of God, the clearer understanding we will have when we hear God speak to our hearts about any problematic situation we may come across. If we do not know what to do, ask God what to do, and if you hear the answer, act on it. If you do not hear God say anything to your spirit or conscience, wait on the Lord until your heart and mind are at peace whether you are the one to help. You may not be the one God wants to use for the situation. This might be hard for some to hear, but God does have other people He has saved in His kingdom who can do as good a job as you can. This is why knowing how to show up is a God-given skill that we practice throughout our lives.

Jesus, Abraham, Job, and many others in the Bible knew how to show up, be accountable, and be full of faith for the problem at hand because they all had a relationship with God the Father. Jesus said, "I only do what I hear my Father tell me." John 5:30 **I can do nothing on my own. I judge as God tells me. Therefore, my judgment is just, because I carry out the will of the one who sent me, not my own will.** Let us enter into a deeper relationship with our God and learn how to show up on God's timetable and within His ability so that God's will be done on earth as it is done in heaven.

Question:

Are you emotionally available when asked to do something you do not want to do or do you panic and wish everyone would leave you alone?

Someone To Blame

Genesis 3:12 And the man said, "The woman whom You gave to be with me—she gave me fruit from the tree, and I ate it."

What is a false flag? *A false flag operation is an act committed with the intent of disguising the actual source of responsibility and pinning the blame on another party.*

Whether by choice or subconsciously, the default setting of the culture we live in has accepted the pinning of blame on other parties as the norm. Blaming all situations for all personal problems one has in life on something or someone else is becoming normal behaviour. If the problems are with our children, spouse, or neighbour the blame is never ours even though we are the common denominator in all the relationships.

Who do you blame when you sin? Who do you blame for all the problems in your family, relationships, or work life? Stop blaming others and let us put the blame and criticism where it belongs: on ourselves. 1John 1:6 **So we are lying if we say we have fellowship with God but go on living in spiritual darkness; we are not practicing the truth.** We need to practice the truth so that the bitterness that results from blame does not permeate our souls and defile our ability to reason with God when He points at what we need to repent for. The hard question I need to ask myself is, why do I plant a false flag when something I missed the mark on is revealed to my heart? Why are the thought lines across my forehead so tight from concentrating on looking for a place to shift the blame for what I have done? Where did the fear of being wrong, or the feeling of accusation come from? When these things are taking place in our hearts, it is most likely that we have lost our peace in Christ. We have stopped resting in the work of the cross. The salvation of our souls has shifted to our altars of self-righteousness and the first sacrifice on that altar is the one you blamed.

Jesus suffered the blame for our sins and He took those sins to the cross He was nailed to. There is no need to rebuild an altar of self-righteous works in our hearts. The Lord has done the finished work of salvation for us, and we only need to surrender to that fact. The Apostle John says it so simply. 1John 1:9 **If we confess our sins, he is faithful and just and will forgive us our sins and purify us from all unrighteousness**. If we confess our sins and not shift the blame of them to others, but take them to the cross we will be forgiven. How have we complicated such a gracious gift? Maybe the issue is that the gift is too wonderful and gracious and our selfish hearts cannot accept so great a sacrifice because we know that if we submit to this amazing love, then there is nothing that Jesus cannot ask of us.

Jesus had two unlikely defenders on the day all the sins and blame of the world were placed upon Him. Pilate's wife warned Pilate not to have anything to do with this innocent man. Matt. 27:19 **While Pilate was sitting on the judgment seat, his wife sent him this message: "Have nothing to do with that innocent man, for I have suffered terribly in a dream today because of Him."** She called Jesus what he was, but the mob could not see His innocence because of the frenzied blame they threw at Him. The thief who was crucified with Christ also spoke up for the Lord's innocence. Luke 23:41 **We are punished justly, because we're getting back what we deserve for the things we did, but this man has done nothing wrong.** The weight of the sins of the world was too great for these two sinful people to deliver Jesus. However, Jesus had all of the authority of the Godhead to deliver mankind from the death that sin had brought into the world.

The thief and Pilate's wife could not deliver Jesus from the wrath that sin had caused within the souls of man because they too needed to be delivered of sin. Sin cannot cast out sin, but righteousness can destroy sin and the iniquities it causes. The world is in turmoil because nations are blaming other nations for the wars, famines, pollution, and greed on the earth. The blame game is within the politics of society. This finger-pointing eventually points back to themselves who are responsible for the laws, rules, and edicts they made. Ahab who was steeped in sin and corruption of every kind blamed Elijah for the problems of Israel. 1Kings 18:17 **When Ahab saw Elijah, Ahab said to him, "Is this you, you troubler of Israel?"** However, Elijah by the Spirit of God pointed out that the false flag Aham was spewing was pure rubbish and that Aham himself was the source of Israel's problems. 1Kings 18:18 **Elijah said, "I have not brought disaster on Israel, but you**

and your father's household have, by abandoning and rejecting the commandments of the LORD and by following the Baals. Ahab was looking for someone to blame, but the blame was totally on the choices being made in his life.

As long as we look for someone to blame for our wrongdoings, mistakes, and outright evil acts, we will remain pathetically immature in the faith. Heb. 5:12 **For though by this time you ought to be teachers because of the time you have had to learn these truths, you actually need someone to teach you again the elementary principles of God's word from the beginning, and you have come to be continually in need of milk, not solid food**. Bitter and sour milk will be our meal of discontent because we refuse to accept responsibility for the false flags we present and the choices we make. Our responsibility in the faith is to answer to God and Him alone. Practising truth and living in it is as much a choice as blaming someone else is also a choice. Growing up in the faith is a choice as remaining immature is a choice. Let us be established in the truth of God by walking with Jesus who is the way, truth, and life, rather than planting a false flag of deception. Let us establish the banner of God over us, which is love.

Questions:

Do you take responsibility for your choices when things go wrong?

_____

Was the above answer true or did you make yourself look good?

_____

God's Invisible Ink

Malachi 3:16 At that time those who feared the LORD spoke to one another. The LORD took notice and listened. So a book of remembrance was written before Him for those who feared the LORD and had high regard for His name.

God writes our story, and much of it is written with invisible ink. We cannot read all the fine details of the account of our existence because the Lord's master plan is much more immense than we can imagine. If we were writing our story our goals would not be large or lofty enough because we would fall for all the regular stuff like riches, fame, and power. The ho-hum human endeavours and life-long goal of owning a fast car, a big house, and a great retirement package would become an ink stain on the story of our life's purpose. There is nothing wrong with these everyday goals, but they are simplistic, earthbound, and temporal, and they become distractions to the infinite reasons we were created. Rev.

4:11 You art worthy, O Lord, to receive glory and honour and power: for you have created all things, and for thy pleasure they are and were created.

When we get out of God's way and allow Him to write our story, then an illiterate man can become a writer or a person born with a deformed leg can become a world track-running Olympian. A woman who cannot bear children becomes the mother and founder of a successful children's orphanage. When God is writing, we are truly living the will of the Godhead. William Wilberforce was a politician to some, but with God inking his thoughts, he became a champion and campaigned to abolish the British slave trade. Florence Nightingale wanted to be a nurse, but when the Lord's hand wrote her story she became the leader of thirty-eight women who volunteered to walk the battlefield and bring healing to the starving and wounded soldiers of the Crimean War. Many people today who have the same spirit and heart as Florence and William are at the tip of the Lord's pen ready to be described in God's words. These are your everyday people who are willing to go out in this lost world and bring Christ along their way by allowing God to write their history. Heb. 12:2a **Let us fix our eyes on Jesus, the author and perfecter of our faith.**

The Bible records many ordinary people who were simply moving along in their day when God's ink started to jot down a different tale that would change their lives forever. Mark 15:21 **And they compelled a passerby, Simon of Cyrene, who was coming in from the country, the father of Alexander and Rufus, to carry his cross.** Simon, the father of two sons, would bring home a story that would be talked about with zeal once the resurrection of Jesus was proclaimed. Who knows what invisible ink was now being written of Rufus and Alexander's life because they had heard of the barbaric cross their father was forced to carry for Jesus? Simon, a countryman, was coming to town to pick up what was needed for the Passover celebration and ended up being written into the story of the Passover Lamb of God.

The Apostle Paul's chronicle was scripted into a living story that would engross readers of the New Testament for centuries to come. God's quill was scribing an eternal narrative of many characters who would become part of the building of the church body of Christ. One of the subplots was about a runaway slave who became one of Paul's helpers while he was in prison. Onesimus was running from a human master only to meet up with the master of the universe and become a slave of value to God and His kingdom. Paul intercedes on behalf of Onesimus and asks Philemon to take him back not just as a slave but as a brother in Christ. Philemon. 1:15 **It seems you lost Onesimus for a little while so that you could have him back forever. 16 He is no longer like a slave to you. He is more than a slave, for he is a beloved brother, especially to me. Now he will mean much more to you, both as a man and as a brother in the Lord.**

Not only did Onesimus come back a born-again brother in Christ, but he returned with Tychicus who would give a true account of what Paul was writing about to the Colossian church. Col. 4:9 **And with him is Onesimus, our faithful and beloved brother, who is one of you. They will let you know everything about the situation here in Rome.** Onesimus ran away as an untrustworthy slave and came back a faithful, redeemed servant, delivering letters that would build the church where Philemon was one of the leaders. The invisible ink of God runs through our stories and we need to let Him write His Word on our hearts so that we may be the catalysts of the Lord's ever-expanding church. There is room for billions more and that story is being written by God the Father.

You might think of yourself as an unlikely character in one of God's eternal stories. This is the lie that Satan wants you to believe because the devil knows the moment you start walking in the narrative God has penned out for you, your ability to destroy the works of the enemy becomes part of your everyday walk in Christ. We are the New Testament story God is writing and we are the people God is using to bring about His kingdom on earth. Jesus said that we walk in a greater privilege and anointing than what came before. Matt. 11:11 **I assure you and most solemnly say to you, among those born of women there has not risen anyone greater than John the Baptist; yet the one who is least in the kingdom of heaven is greater in privilege than he.** How can we not let God write our stories? He is the master author of all history and if we submit to the will of God we will be written into the narrative God has chosen. May it be said of us that we were a blessing to write about.

Questions:

What would you like God to write into your story for this next part of your life?

_____

Have you talked with God about becoming a better version of yourself?

_____

What is God asking you to do to help your story become an epic volume of hope?

_____

About The Author

I have been in Christian ministry in one form or another for about forty years. I attended Commonwealth Bible College in Katoomba, New South Wales, Australia, in 1980. During that time I was involved in prison ministries, exhorting the Gospel on the radio in a small town, and church-related service of all kinds. I have taught bible college courses and also have been involved in personal discipleship training.

God has blessed me all along the way. Now I have the opportunity to write down what was experienced throughout the years. The Lord has blessed me with sound and forthright material to write a series of Christian devotionals. I have lived the testimonies on these pages and can attest to the fact that God is so faithful and good.

Connect With Norm

Norm's Blog can now be found online in
English, French and Spanish.
Your comments on any of the hundreds of
blog posts are appreciated.
English sirnorm.com
French sirnorm.com/fr/
Spanish sirnorm.com/es/